Dorothea Hall is a freelance writer and editor with a background in textiles and teaching. During her career she has designed textiles and wallpapers for the major London manufacturers; has taught art and crafts and lectured on interior design — a subject in which she finds constant inspiration; was the Stichery Editor of Busy Needles.

Dorothea has edited, written and contributed to numerous books on crafts and interior style. Her most recent publications are Nursery Rhymes in Cross Stitch, Fairy Tales in Cross Stitch, Cross stitch for Children, Cross Stitch for the Home, Quick and Easy Cross Stitch and Cross Stitch for Special Occasions.

A DESIGN EYE BOOK

First published in 1992 by Blitz Editions,
an imprint of Bookmart Limited, Registered Number 2372865.
Trading as Bookmart Limited, Desford Road, Enderby, Leicester, LE9 5AD

ISBN 1 85605 068 8

Printed in China

With special thanks to T.C.Li.

Design Eye Ltd, 8 Fouberts Place, London W1V 1HH.

CONTENTS

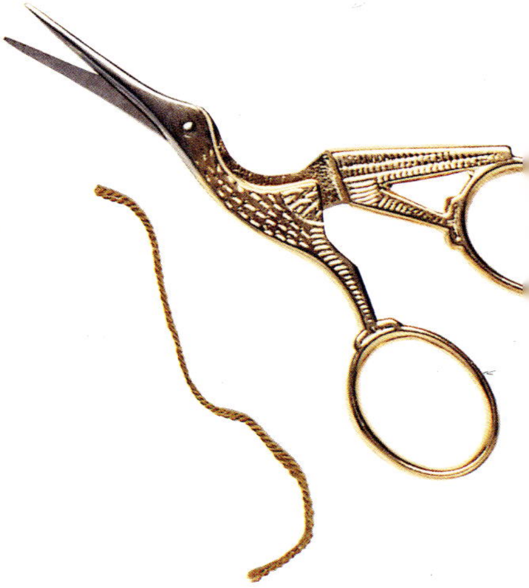

Illustrations by *Harry Harrison*

Photography by *Paul Forrester*
Chas Wilder

Introduction

In recent years the image of needlecrafts has become extremely attractive, designer–led and fashionable. Needlework shops and general stores are suddenly full of stock showing a wonderful array of colourful yarns, threads fabrics and kits. As a result there are now many people who would like to know how to do these needlecrafts but are, perhaps, put off partly because of the mystique that has been associated with acquiring needlework skills, and because instructions can sometimes look impossibly complicated. In fact, none of the basic skills involved is at all difficult to learn – all that is required is a willingness to try, a little time and patience.

The book begins by discussing the equipment and the basic skills you will need. It describes the different types of fabrics and threads, frames, needles, and general accessories that are common to all fabric crafts with information on what they are used for. Full explanations are also given on how to enlarge designs, transfer patterns and how to stretch fabric over cardboard ready for display.

The following eight chapters include the most popular needlecrafts and are arranged with the simplest form of embroidery first, progressing to more challenging types – although there is no reason why even a beginner should not start anywhere in the book. Beginning with counted thread embroidery, where quite complicated-looking designs can easily be achieved using only a single colour, the text explains the different types within the group (darning, double-running and counted satin stitch patterns) and suggests ways of practising the embroidery by experimenting with patterns and stitches. The chapter ends with full instructions for making the main project - three lavender sachets each with a different counted thread motif on the front.

The needlecrafts chosen fall into two broad categories: the first, which includes counted thread, cross stitch, cutwork, surface embroidery and needlepoint, are embroidery crafts whereas quilting, patchwork and appliqué are fabric crafts – each one involving quite different disciplines. However, once you have mastered one or two of the basic disciplines, it should not be too difficult to re-interpret the projects using your own ideas – mixing embroidery with patchwork and appliqué, for example.

The book shows a wide range of projects and motifs – illustrating both traditional and contemporary styles. At the same time as learning the basic skills, the reader is given the opportunity to create some of the most beautiful needlecrafts of our time.

BEFORE YOU BEGIN

Note that charts and trace patterns required for working the projects are given at the back of the book. A page reference is given at the beginning of each project.

Where charts are given for working counted thread, cross stitch and needlepoint, the designs are represented by symbols on a grid, and some readers may find it helpful to have the chart enlarged so that the symbols can be seen more easily. Many photocopying services will do this for a nominal charge. Indeed, where a linear trace pattern is given on a graph, you can always have that enlarged in the same way, following the appropriate scale given with the trace pattern.

Extra fabric has been added to allow for preparing the edges (particularly on evenweave fabrics that are liable to fray) and for stretching it in a frame.

When you begin to work a design, remember to match the centre lines given on the diagram (shown by small arrows) and the basting stitches on your fabric, and use them as reference points for centring your design accurately.

For patchwork and appliqué, it is a good idea to wash and press all the fabrics first, to test for shrinkage and colour fastness.

CHAPTER
•ONE•

Equipment & Basic Skills

The basic equipment needed for the following needlecrafts is fairly simple and can be bought at most needlework stores. While some items, such as fabrics, threads and frames, are used for all types of embroidery and fabric crafts, it is helpful to know which particular pieces of equipment are used for specific tasks to give the best results.

Fabrics

In general, fabrics can be divided into three groups depending on their structure; evenweave, non-evenweave and bonded.

EVENWEAVE fabrics are traditionally used for all counted thread embroidery such as pattern darning, counted satin stitch, double running stitch (blackwork) and cross stitch. Evenweave is fabric with the same number of threads counted in both directions over, for example, 2.5cm (1in). This includes linens, Hardanger, huckaback, Zweigart's Aida, Linda, Lugano and Tula. These fabrics are available in a variety of weights ranging from fine [40 threads to 2.5cm (1in)] to coarse [10 threads to 2.5cm (1in)], and in a wide range of colours. Although linens are produced in a relatively limited range of weights and colours, and tend to be expensive, they can be bought from most specialist suppliers.

From left to right, evenweaves: linens, Hardanger, Zweigart's Linda, Davosa and Aida, needlepoint canvases; non-evenweaves; calico, lawn muslin and sateen; bonded fabrics: iron-on interfacing, felt, synthetic wadding and loose wadding.

The more popular, and less expensive, evenweaves include the previously mentioned Zweigart's range of cotton and cotton and synthetic mixes. These particular fabrics can also be recognized by their distinctive weave. Where, for example, ordinary linens have a single weave, Hardanger has a double weave and huckaback is woven in groups of threads which form a pronounced checked effect. Similarly, Aida and Tula have a checked effect (the advantage being that the holes are easier to count) whereas Linda and Lugano are of single-weave construction.

CANVAS is an evenweave upon which needlepoint is worked – mostly in yarn – and the entire surface is covered with interlocking stitches.

This fabric is much heavier than other evenweaves, and is made from polished linen or cotton threads in either single- or double-thread canvas; double-threads can be split to make finer stitches in specific areas, such as the features on a face. It is produced in a variety of counts and widths ranging from 10 to 32 threads to 2.5cm (1in) single canvas to 7 to 18 threads to 2.5cm (1in) double canvas, in either antique (brown) or white. Choose antique for working dark colours and white for light colours.

NON-EVENWEAVE fabrics are mostly used for patchwork, quilting and appliqué, and for many types of surface embroidery. Smooth, closely woven fabrics such as dressweight cottons, brushed cotton, lightweight wool, lawn, poplin, satin, silk sateen or even very fine linens are best for quilting and patchwork, while an additional mixture of heavier tweeds and laces may be used for an appliqué picture, for example, to give a realistic effect.

BONDED fabrics include all types of felts, cotton and synthetic waddings. Felt can be used for appliqué projects, toys and so on, and is available in a vast range of colours and thicknesses. It can be bought by the metre or in small handy pieces. Synthetic and cotton wadding is used as an interlining in both patchwork and quilting. Synthetic wadding is lightweight and washable. It comes in standard widths and thicknesses and is made up in layers, which means that it can be separated to suit individual needs. The 56g (2oz), 112g (4oz) and 224g (8oz) weights are most popular.

Cotton wadding tends to move and separate during washing which means that it should be closely quilted. Being heavier than synthetic wadding, it is ideal for hangings. Loose polyester or cotton fibre is particularly useful for filling cushions or pads made to your own dimensions.

Threads

There is an enormous range of threads available and while many may be intermixed successfully in experimental work, for the purposes of this book, those that are produced for a specific purpose are discussed.

Generally speaking, your choice of thread should be determined by your choice of fabric – bearing in mind that you can either match the thread to the fabric – silk thread to silk fabric; the weight of thread to the weight of fabric; or use a thread suited to a particular purpose, such as quilting thread.

Six-stranded embroidery thread *is loosely twisted, mercerized cotton with a slight sheen used mostly for surface embroidery. It is available in a wide variety of colours in both plain and random-dyed effects.*

Coton à broder *is a single, medium-twisted thread with a shiny finish and is available in many colours. This thread is used for cutwork, hemstitching, counted thread and surface embroidery.*

Pearl cotton *is a single thread with a well-defined twist and shiny finish. This is available in several thicknesses and in both plain and random-dyed colours. It is used as for coton à broder.*

Linen thread *is a very strong and tightly twisted single thread with a slight lustrous finish, available in varying thicknesses and a limited range of colours. It is traditionally used for cut-work hemstitching and other forms of embroidery.*

Filo floss *is a soft, loosely twisted, six-stranded pure silk thread which can easily be separated and used in single or varying multiple strands as required. It is available in a vast range of colours and used almost solely for surface embroidery.*

Soft embroidery cotton *is a single, fairly thick soft thread with a matt finish. It comes in a wide range of colours and is used for coarser forms of surface embroidery.*

Quilting thread *is smoother and stronger than ordinary cotton sewing threads and is available in a limited range of colours. Alternatively, use No. 50 or 60 heavy-duty mercerized cotton for quilting.*

No. 60 cotton sewing thread *is recommended for hand- or machine-sewn patchwork, and is available in a variety of colours.*

General-purpose sewing threads *of the cotton/polyester type are used for appliqué. They come in an enormous range of colours but tend to knot and fray in hand sewing. Like any other hand-sewing thread, they can be drawn through beeswax to prevent them from twisting and to strengthen them.*

Crewel wool *is a very fine, firmly twisted 2-ply yarn which can be used for surface embroidery or for needlepoint. It is available in a range of 'antique' colours and can be used singly or in multiple strands.*

Tapestry wool *is a softly twisted yarn, similar to a 4-ply yarn which can be used for surface embroidery or for needlepoint. It is available in an excellent range of colours and is used for needlepoint embroidery.*

Persian yarn *is a loosely twisted yarn made up of three 2-ply strands which can be separated and used singly or in varying numbers of strands. It is available in an enormous range of colours and is used for needlepoint.*

A selection of embroidery threads and yarns, needles and sewing accessories.

Needles

In general, choose a needle with an eye that is large enough to hold the thread and yet small enough to pass easily through the fabric without distorting it.

Crewel needles *have sharp points and long oval eyes and should be used for fine to medium-weight embroidery. They are available in size 1-10.*

Chenille needles *have sharp points, large oval eyes and are bigger than crewel needles. They are used for embroidering with coarser threads and fabrics, and are also available in several sizes, ranging from 18-24.*

Tapestry needles *have large oval eyes and rounded points. They are used for needlepoint and embroidery on evenweave fabrics, and are available in sizes 18-26.*

Sharps, quilting needles and betweens *are all round-eyed and sharp-pointed and are used for hand sewing. Quilting needles are the shortest in length, about 2.5cm (1in).*

Frames

Rectangular frames and hoops are used to support the ground fabric while stitching. Although a frame is not absolutely essential there are positive advantages to using one for all counted thread, surface embroidery, appliqué and needlepoint; note that needlepoint canvas can only be mounted in a rectangular frame.

A frame will keep the fabric evenly stretched and prevent it from becoming distorted. This can so easily happen when working in the hand, especially when cross stitches and needlepoint stitches, for example, are made by 'scooping' the fabric. If the frame is supported, this will leave both hands free to stitch – with one hand on top and the other below, the correct up and down movements can be made. Rectangular frames and large quilting hoops can be used for small pieces of quilting and appliqué, but for very large items a quilting frame is recommended.

General Accessories

In addition to the items already mentioned, you will also need a pair of dressmaker's shears for cutting out; a pair of sharp-pointed small embroidery scissors for snipping into seams and neatening threads; a pair of general purpose scissors for cutting paper and card; a tape measure; basting thread; stainless steel pins; an iron and ironing board; ruler and pencil.
A sewing machine is useful for making up items in all fabric crafts, especially on large projects, where it will give a stronger seam and also help to speed up the finishing process.

Basic Skills

Refer to the basic skills given below when making the projects in the book.

USING A HOOP A hoop consists of two rings, usually made from wood, which fit closely one inside the other. The outer ring has a screw attachment, so that the tension of the fabric can be adjusted and held firmly in place.

Hoops with table- or floor-stands attached are available in sizes, ranging from 10cm (4in) in diameter to quilting hoops 61cm (24in) in diameter.

1 Before stretching your fabric in the hoop, bind both rings with bias binding to stop the fabric from slipping (especially necessary with silky fabrics) and to prevent the rings from marking the fabric.

2 Place the area of fabric to be embroidered over the inner ring with a layer of tissue paper on top to prevent the outer ring from marking the fabric (optional). Press the outer ring over it with the tension screw released.

3 Smooth the fabric and, if necessary, straighten the grain before tightening the screw. Tear away the paper from the centre of the ring to expose the fabric ready for embroidering.

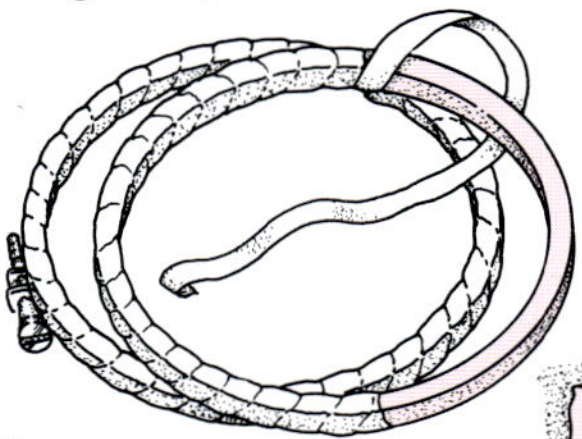

1

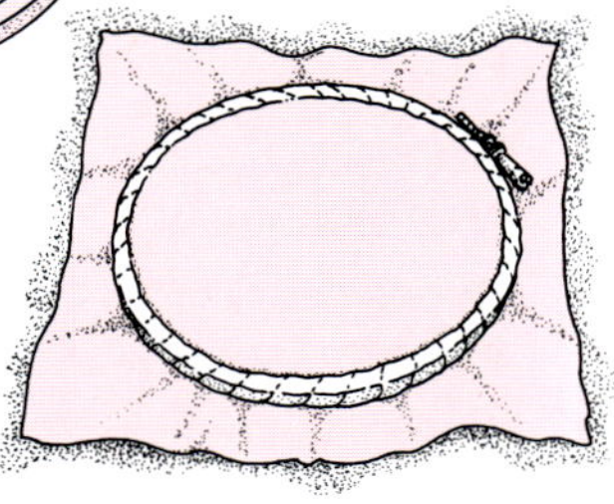

2

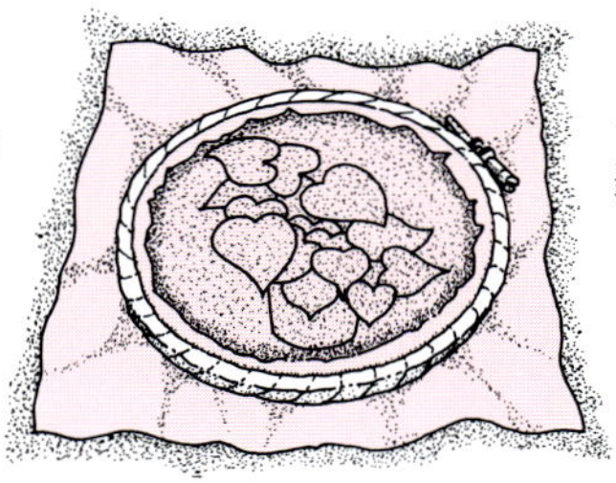

3

USING A RECTANGULAR FRAME Rectangular frames consist of two rollers with tapes attached, and two stretchers which slot into the rollers and are held firmly in place by pegs or screw attachments. These are adjusted to give the right amount of tension to the fabric, after it has been laced to the sides.

Frames are measured across the width of the roller tape, and are available in several sizes, ranging from 30cm (12in) to 68cm (27in) and may be fitted with either table- or floor-stands.

1 To stretch your fabric in a frame, first cut the fabric to size, allowing an extra 5cm (2in) all round the finished size of the embroidery. Baste a single 1cm ($^3/_8$in) hem on the top and bottom edges and oversew a length of webbing or strong tape, 2.5cm (1in) wide, to the other two sides. Using contrasting thread, mark the centre both ways with basting stitches.

2 Working from the centre outwards, pin the top and bottom edges to the roller tapes and then, using strong thread, oversew them in place. Fit the side pieces through the slots and roll any excess fabric onto one roller until the fabric is taut.

3 Insert the pegs or adjust the screws to tighten the frame. Using a chenille needle threaded with strong thread or fine string, lace both edges through the webbing and around the frame, stitching at 2.5cm (1in) intervals, and stretching the fabric evenly. Secure the ends around the intersections of the frame.

1

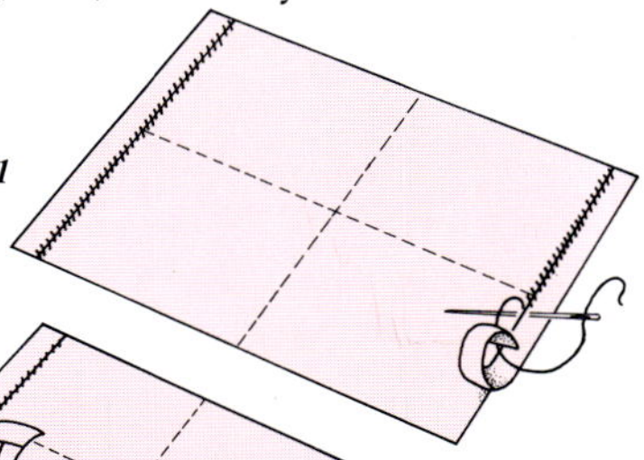

2

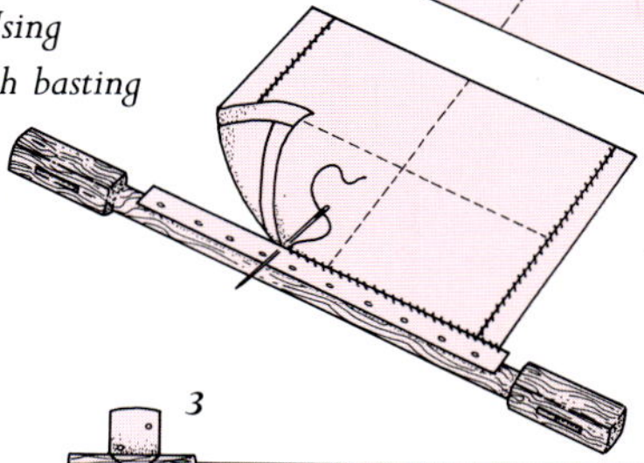

3

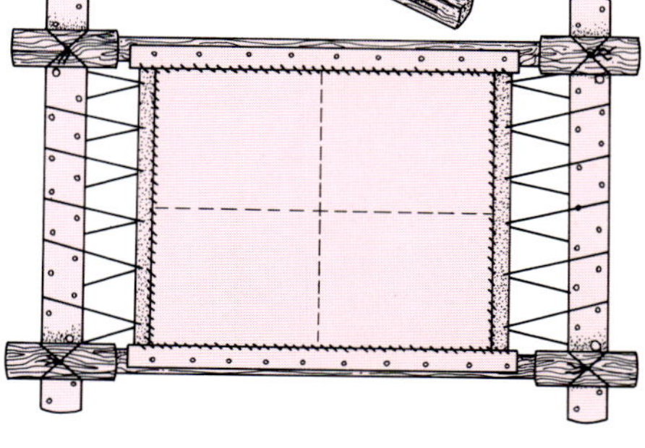

ENLARGING A GRAPH PATTERN A number of designs in this book are shown as graph patterns, which means that they must first be enlarged to the correct size before they can be transferred to fabric. The scale of the full-sized pattern is given on the appropriate page, for example: 'Each square = 5cm (2in)'. This means that each small square on the printed diagram should correspond to a 5cm (2in) square on your enlarged grid.

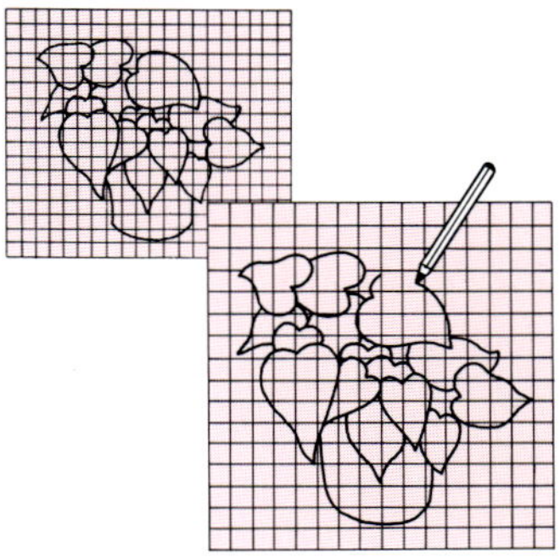

To enlarge a graph pattern, you will need a sheet of graph paper ruled in 1cm (3/8in) squares, a ruler or pencil. Where, for example, the scale given is one square equals 5cm (2in), you should mark your grid with 5cm (2in) squares. Copy the graph freehand from the small grid to the larger one, completing one square at a time. Use a ruler to draw the straight lines first, and then copy the freehand curves.

TRANSFERRING A DESIGN The simplest way to transfer a design to fabric is by using dressmaker's carbon paper. This can be bought in several colours, which means that you can choose a light colour (white or yellow) for dark fabrics, and a dark colour (red or blue) for light colours. This method is suitable for embroidery fabric with a relatively smooth surface.

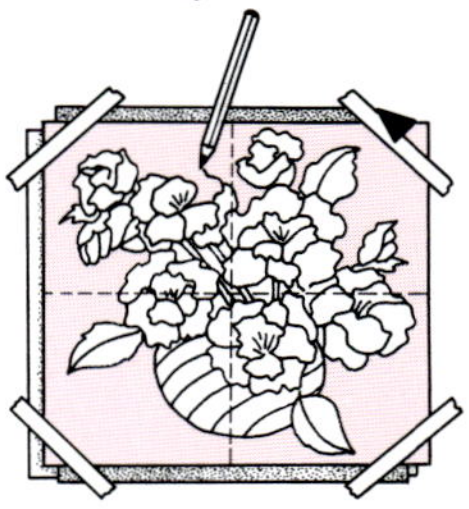

Working on a clean, firm surface, lay the fabric right-side up. Place the carbon paper face-down with the traced design on top, and secure it at the corners with masking tape. Using a pencil, draw around the outline, pressing firmly to transfer a clear outline.

MOUNTING EMBROIDERY You can give pictures and other similar projects a professional finish by mounting them over cardboard before framing. Lightweight fabrics can be attached at the back with pieces of masking tape, while heavier fabrics are best laced across the back in the traditional way.

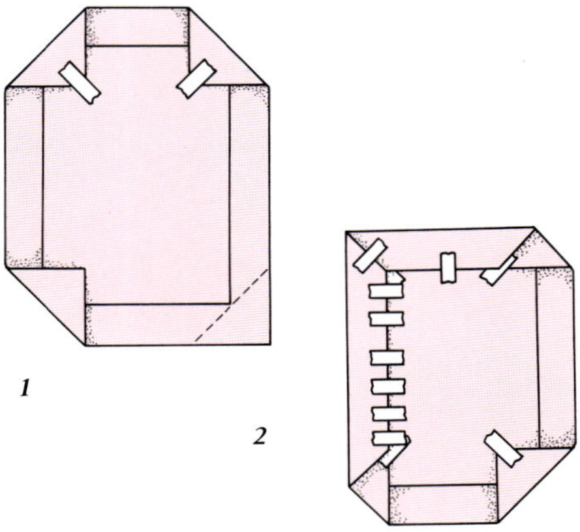

1 Cut the cardboard to the size of the picture plus 6mm (1/4in) all round to allow for the recess in the picture frame. To help centre the cardboard over the embroidery, it is useful to mark the centre of the cardboard both ways with a faint pencil line. Similarly, mark the centre of the embroidery both ways with pins or basting stitches. Working on a clean surface, place the embroidery face-down, with the cardboard centred over it and matching the centre lines. Fold over the corners of the fabric and secure with pieces of masking tape. Remove the pins. Always work on opposite sides.

*2 In the case of **lightweight** fabrics, secure the sides and the mitred corners with pieces of masking tape placed about 2.5cm (1in) apart.*

*3 For **heavier** fabrics, fold over the edges of the fabric, and lace across using strong thread. Repeat on the other two sides. Fold each corner into a mitre. Pull up the lacing fairly tightly, stretching the fabric evenly. Finally, overstitch the corners.*

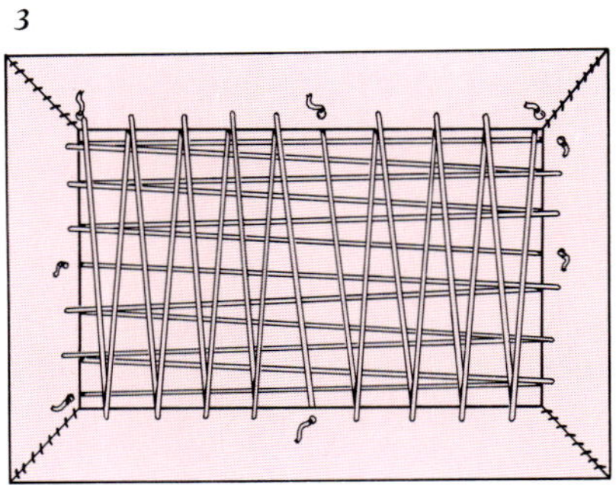

CHAPTER
•TWO•

Counted Thread Embroidery

Counted thread embroidery, as its name implies, is stitched on an evenweave fabric that has easily countable threads, as the regularity of the stitching is most important to the finished effect. Several types of embroidery are included in this category, the simplest being pattern darning, double running stitch (blackwork) and counted satin stitch.

PATTERN DARNING is worked in parallel rows of straight stitches, in varying lengths, so as to form a pattern on the surface of the ground fabric. The designs are worked out on graph paper, and can be used for backgrounds, borders and spot motifs. The basic darning stitch is worked in the same way as running stitch and, by varying the numbers of threads that are both picked up and stitched over, many intricate patterns can be made using a single colour. However, by adding colours, more complicated patterns can be made, similar to the early nineteenth century designs which simulated intricately woven cloth.

Following the stitch diagrams and the diaper patterns given below, and using a round-ended tapestry needle, experiment first using single colours – and then, for a more intricate effect, add a second colour to the patterns.

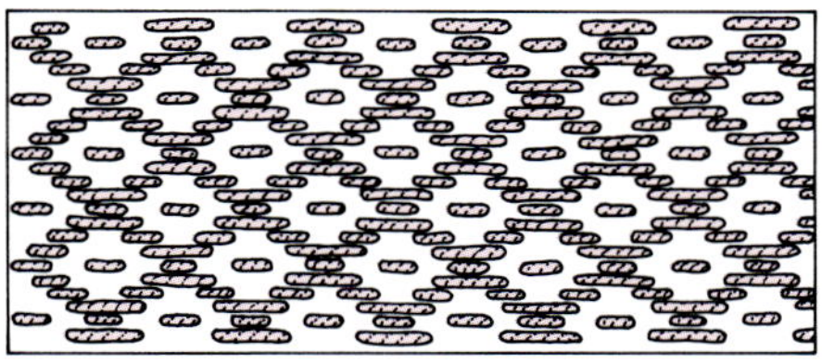

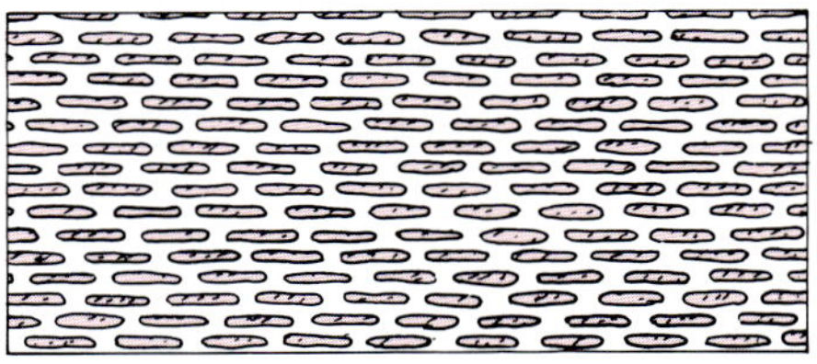

To make a lavender sachet with a darned motif, see page 14.

DARNING STITCH Work this simple darning stitch in a similar way to tacking stitch. Depending on the coarseness of the fabric, keep the length of the stitch to within 1cm (3/8in).

Begin at the right-hand side and pick up one thread only between each stitch. Place the stitches of the second and subsequent rows directly beneath the picked-up thread to make a neat 'brick' filling.

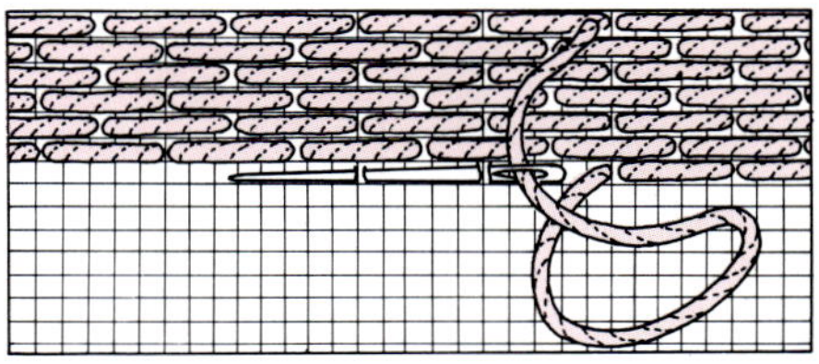

DOUBLE RUNNING STITCH (or blackwork) embroidery is worked in a single colour – traditionally in black or red – and the patterns are made up entirely of delicate lines, giving a beautiful filigree effect. Simple designs can be planned on graph paper and used as for pattern darning.

Double running stitch is very simple to work (see the diagram below) and should look the same on both sides of the fabric. While many traditional designs are geometric and linear, blackwork designs today may be more experimental – where natural subjects are interpreted in different stitch patterns to give the impression of shaded etchings or drawings.

Working from right to left, embroider a row of running stitches by passing the needle over and under two threads (or the specific number your pattern requires), following the design. At the end of each row, turn the embroidery around, and work a second row of running stitches along the same line, filling in the spaces left.

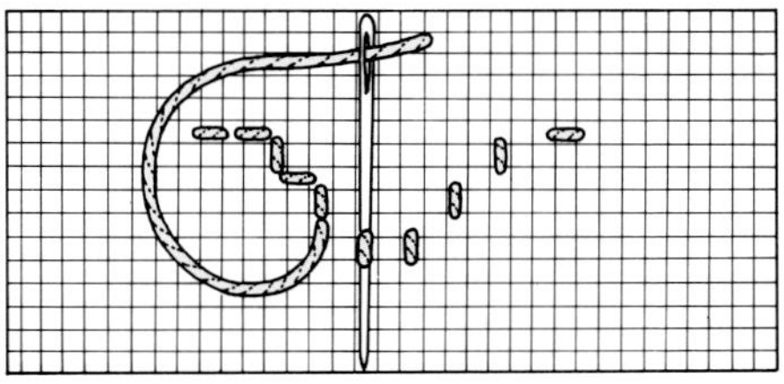

Following the stitch diagram and the patterns given below, experiment with these simple designs using one or two colours only.

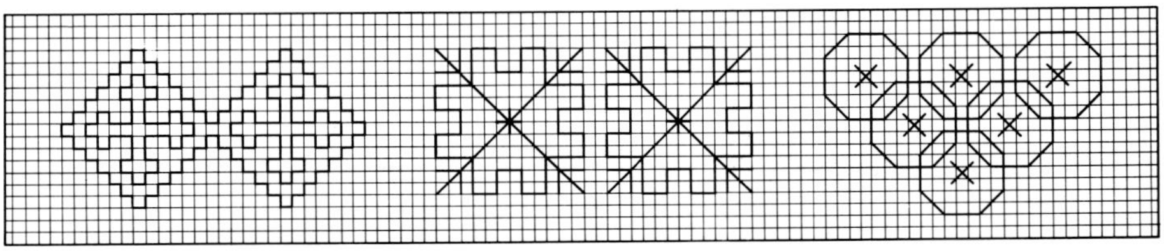

To make a lavender sachet with a double running stitch motif, see page 14.

COUNTED SATIN STITCH as its name implies, consists of satin stitch embroidered over a given number of threads to form individual geometric patterns. The designs are made up of vertical, horizontal or diagonal flat stitches and usually form fairly solid blocks of pattern. These patterns are usually worked in one or two colours only, but you could experiment by introducing more colours and by mixing any of the examples given below into larger repeat patterns or borders.

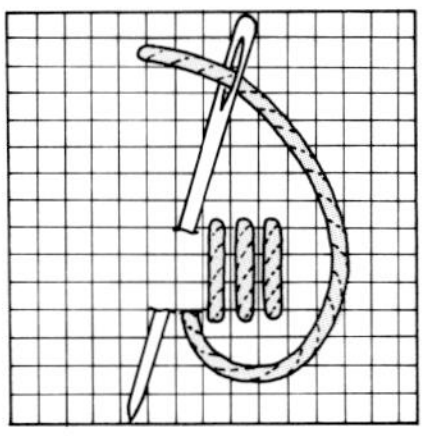

Working either from left to right or right to left, stitch over 4 threads (or the required number to suit your pattern sequence).

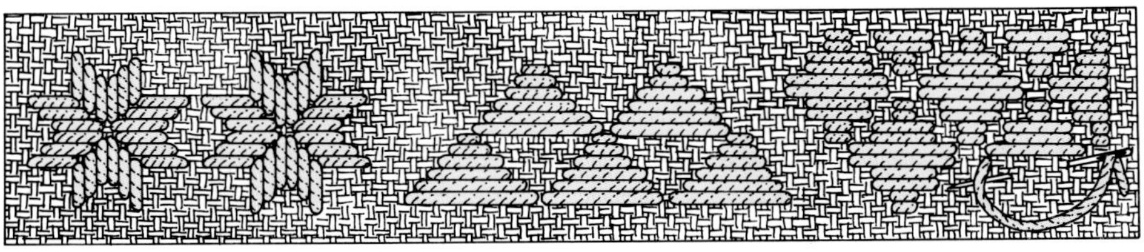

To make a lavender sachet with a counted satin stitch motif, see page 14.

Lacy Lavender Sachets

For one sachet, with an overall measurement of 18cm x 11cm (7in x 4½in), you will need:

- **41cm x 15cm (16in x 6in) of white openweave fabric, such as Davosa, 18 threads to 2.5cm (1in)**
- **25cm (10in) of pre-gathered white broderie anglaise trim, 3cm (1¼in) wide**
- **46cm (18in) of white satin ribbon, 1cm (⅜in) wide**
- **1 skein of DMC stranded embroidery cotton in the colour given with the chart, see page I**
- **No 26 tapestry needle**
- **Matching sewing thread**
- **Lavender or pot pourri to half-fill the sachet**

THE EMBROIDERY In order to centre the motif, you will need to transfer the positioning lines to the embroidery fabric. Fold the fabric in half widthways and mark this line with pins. Measure 2.5cm (1in) in from this point and baste across. This is the baseline for the motif. Baste the upright centre line.

With the fabric lightly held in a hoop, follow the appropriate chart and stitch diagram and complete the motif, using four strands of thread in the needle for the pattern darning, two strands for double back stitch and three strands for counted satin stitch. Remove the basting stitches and steam press the finished embroidery on the wrong side.

MAKING UP THE SACHET With the right sides together, fold the fabric in half widthways; baste and machine stitch the sides, taking a 2cm (¾in) seam. Trim the seam allowances to 1cm (⅜in), and turn to the right side. Make a single 5cm (2in) turning on the top edge and baste.

Join the short edges of the lace trim, using a tiny French seam. Pin and baste the trim to the inside of the top edge and, working from the right side, machine stitch in place, sewing close to the top edge. Half-fill the sachet with lavender or pot pourri and tie the ribbon around the top, finishing with the bow in front.

Sweet smelling lavender sachets to please any reader. Each has a single–coloured motif in counted thread embroidery, and the bag is delicately edged with lace trim and tied with a shiny satin bow.

CHAPTER
•THREE•

Cross Stitch

Cross stitch is usually worked on an evenweave fabric, where the background remains unstitched; or it is worked on canvas where the stitches cover the ground completely, see Equipment page 7. Being one of the oldest forms of embroidery, cross stitch along with satin stitch and chain stitch (and their numerous variations) are also found in embroideries around the world. Styles can vary enormously from intricate geometric patterns to flowing naturalistic designs.

CHARTING YOUR OWN NATURALISTIC DESIGN Using graph paper and coloured crayons, it is perhaps easier than it looks to chart such a cross stitch design. You may be inspired by a favourite painting or botanical illustration, for example, but one thing to bear in mind is that it should not be too fine nor too detailed, and the underside should be plain and unprinted.

If you have access to a light-box, tape the illustration to the glass; if not, to a window pane, and centre the graph paper on top. You can then either outline the design with pencil, remove it from the glass and fill in each square using the appropriate coloured crayon; or, using a fine black pen, fill in each square of the design with a symbol to represent each colour. Make a colour key on the chart and match each colour used in the original design to an embroidery thread, making a note of its number, in case you need to buy more. See also Designs for needlepoint, page 31.

In addition to cross stitch, use backstitch to outline an area or to emphasize a fold of fabric or veins on a leaf, for example; and use half a cross stitch to delineate finer detail.

CROSS STITCH For all cross stitch embroidery, the following two methods of working are used. In each case, neat rows of vertical stitches are produced on the back of the fabric.

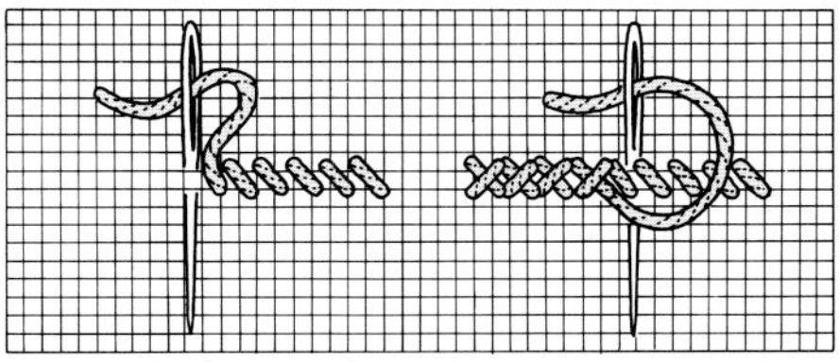

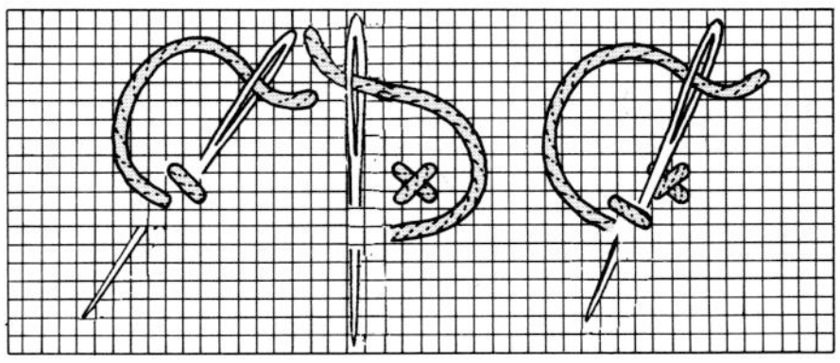

1 When stitching large areas, work in horizontal rows. Working from right to left, complete the first row of evenly spaced diagonal stitches over the number of threads specified in the instructions. Then, working from left to right, repeat the process. Continue in this way, making sure each stitch and successive rows cross in the same direction. 2 When working diagonal lines, small areas, and single stitches, work downwards completing each stitch before moving on to the next.

BACK STITCH Backstitch, used in cross stitch embroidery to emphasize a foldline or shadow, for example, should be worked over the same number of threads as the cross stitch, and form continuous straight or diagonal lines.

Make the first stitch left to right; pass the needle behind the fabric and bring it out one stitch length ahead to the left. Repeat and continue in this way along the line.

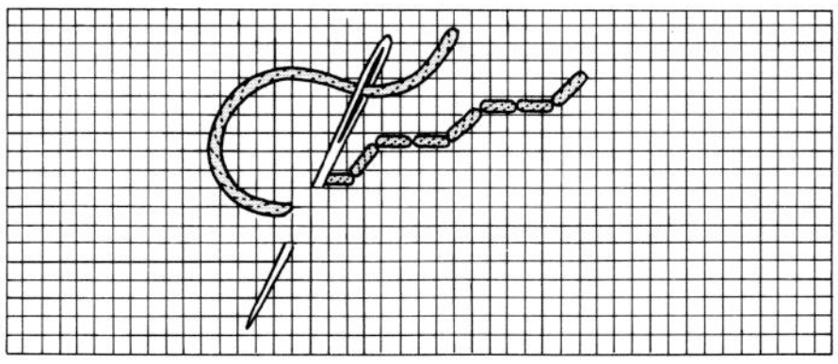

If you are a beginner to cross stitch embroidery, you may prefer to work a practice piece copying a few simple geometric patterns picked out from the traditional motifs shown opposite, before moving on to the lace-edged bookmarks with their naturalistic designs, see page 18.

HEMSTITCH When working Aida and similar fabrics, it is not necessary to remove any threads as a guideline for stitching since the lines between the square blocks can easily be seen.

Bring the needle out on the right side, one square below the stitchline. Working from left to right, pick up two blocks/squares as shown in the diagram. Bring the needle out again and insert it behind the fabric, to emerge one square down, ready to make the next stitch. Before reinserting the needle, pull the thread tight, so that the bound threads are held firm.

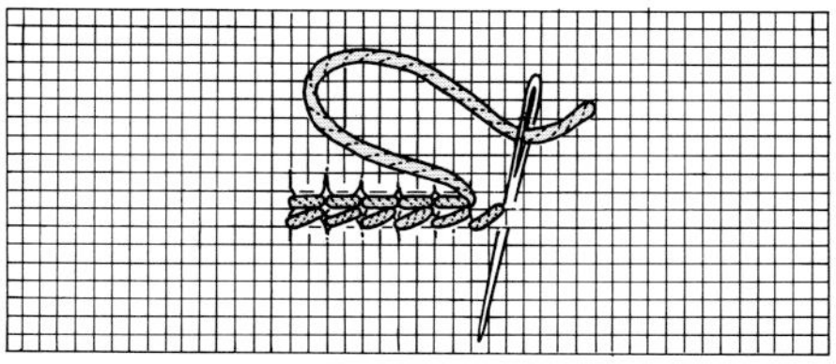

Cross Stitch Bookmarks and Pincushion

Dragonfly Bookmark and Pincushion The fabric and threads supplied with the book are sufficient to make either the bookmark or the pincushion; to adapt the design to fit the pincushion, see the chart on page **II**. In addition to the fabric and threads supplied, you will need sufficient loose synthetic wadding to fill the cushion.

NOTE Where there is relatively little embroidery involved, such as in a bookmark or the pincushion, you may find that working in the hand does not present too much of a problem with keeping the tension even. However, you can quite easily stitch oddments of cotton fabric to the four edges of a prepared or evenweave bookmark which will enable you to stretch it in a hoop.

MAKING THE BOOKMARK Press the fabric, and trim one long edge by 1.5cm (5/8 in). Baste the centre both ways. Following the chart and using four strands of thread in the needle supplied, complete the cross stitching working in the hand. Use two strands of thread for backstitching the central 3012 leaf and the dark eyes on the dragonfly wings. Backstitch a double outline around the embroidery, working one stitch over one square, and using two strands of white thread in the needle.

Following the stitch diagram (page 17), hemstitch around the edge, working next to the backstitch border, and taking each stitch over two squares across by one square deep. Damp press the embroidery on the wrong side, and then withdraw the threads to complete the fringing.

MAKING THE PINCUSHION With the pressed fabric placed horizontally, first baste the vertical centre and then baste vertical lines 21 squares in from each side. These second lines mark the centre of the embroidery and allow for a hem at each side, three squares deep.

Following the instructions given on the chart, complete the two halves of the embroidery, using the same number of strands in the needle supplied as for the bookmark.

Pretty and practical! Each bookmark is finished with a delicate edging.

Using two strands of white thread in the needle, backstitch vertical rows at each side of the embroidery. Work the first two rows next to the embroidery and then miss one line. Repeat this sequence until you have worked four double rows at each side.

With right sides together, fold the fabric in half and then backstitch around the edges leaving a 5cm opening in one side, making them 3 squares deep. Trim across the corners, turn through to the right side and press. Fill with wadding and slipstitch the opening to close. Remove the basting stitches.

For the tassels, thread two 9cm (3in) lengths of white thread (six strands) through the tip of each corner and knot together. Trim the threads to 2cm ($\frac{3}{4}$in).

For ***The Bee and Dandelion*** and ***The Butterfly and Vetch bookmarks,*** you will need:

- **One cream and one white prepared lace-edged bookmark, 18 threads to 2.5cm (1in), each bookmark is 5cm (2in) wide (for suppliers, see page 48)**
- **DMC stranded embroidery cotton in the colours given with the appropriate charts on page II**
- **No 26 tapestry needle**

THE EMBROIDERY Baste the centre lines and then, following the stitch diagrams and referring to the appropriate chart, complete the embroidery using two strands in the needle throughout. Remember to match the centre lines on the chart with the basting stitches on the bookmark, to position your embroidery. Remove the bookmarks from the hoop, take out all basting threads and, if needed, steam press on the wrong side.

Cutwork

This is a delicate and lacy form of embroidery, in which parts of the background fabric are cut away to emphasize the design. There are several types of cutwork, the simplest consisting of 'cut away' areas outlined in buttonhole stitch, while more complicated examples (known as Renaissance and Richelieu) have additional decorative bars and picots respectively.

Successful cutwork depends entirely on a well-planned design, where it is essential to have all the main points attached – and where larger areas are to be cut away, bars and branched bars are made to link the edges so as to avoid loose sections appearing when the background is cut away.

All the main outlines of cutwork designs should be drawn double, about 3mm (1/8 in) wide; these act as guidelines for the buttonhole stitching, and are first outlined in running stitch. Designs can be transferred to fabric using dressmaker's carbon paper, see page 11. Where bars have been added to a design, they should be completed at the same time as the running stitches – before the buttonhole stitching is worked and the background cut away.

For best results, it is essential to choose a closely woven fabric with an even texture, such as fine linen or cotton. For the embroidery, use a crewel needle, and either coton à broder or stranded cotton in two or three strands, depending on the weight of the fabric. You will also need a pair or sharp-pointed embroidery scissors for cutting into angles and around curves.

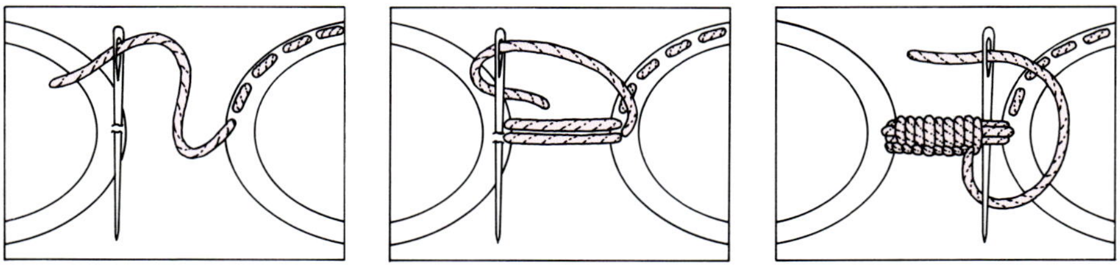

***PLAIN BAR 1** Continue to outline the design with running stitch. At the point where a bar is planned, take the needle across to the opposite side and make a small stitch. **2** Return the needle to the opposite side and make a similar stitch. Depending on the thickness of your thread and the weight of the bar needed, take a third thread across and anchor it as before. **3** Cover the bar neatly with buttonhole stitches, keeping the bar flat and detached from the fabric. Return to the starting point and continue until the next bar is reached.*

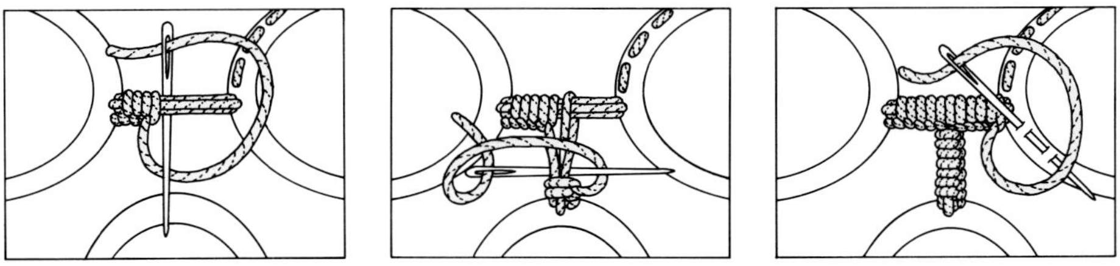

BRANCHED BAR 1 *Use a branched bar to link three motifs. Work as for steps 1 and 2 of a plain bar, then buttonhole stitch to the centre of the bar.* ***2*** *Take the needle across to the third motif and make a small stitch, then take it around the centre of the first bar and back again, making a small stitch. Buttonhole to the centre of the first bar.* ***3*** *Complete buttonhole stitching the first bar, then continue to outline the motif until the next bar is reached.*

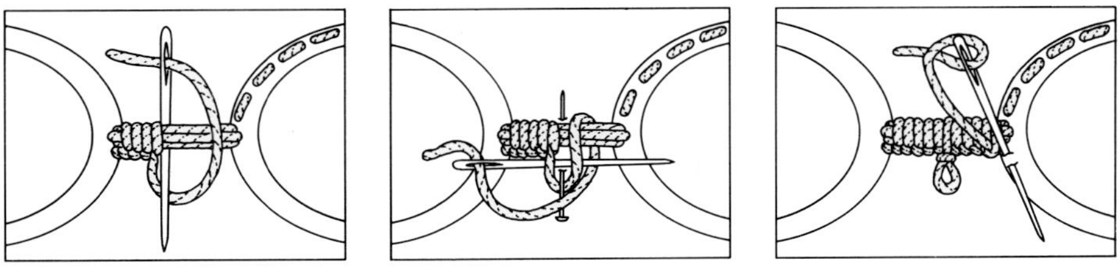

SIMPLE PICOT BAR 1 *Work as for steps 1 and 2 of a plain bar. Buttonhole stitch to the centre of the bar. Insert a pin into the fabric beneath, as shown in step 2.* ***2*** *Loop the thread under the pin head from left to right. Pass the needle behind the bar and pull through. Re-insert it under the loop of the pin and bring it out with the thread under the needle point.* ***3*** *Pull the thread tight to secure the picot. Remove the pin, and complete the bar with an equal number of stitches. Continue with running stitch to the next bar.*

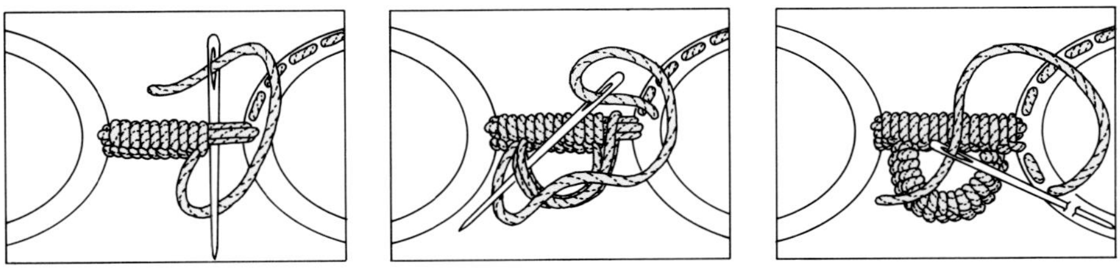

SCALLOPED BAR 1 *Work steps 1 and 2 of a plain bar. Buttonhole stitch almost to the end of the bar.* ***2*** *Pass the needle back and forth through the looped edge of the stitching and over the bar to make the foundation threads for the scallop.* ***3*** *Buttonhole stitch around the scallop, keeping it flat and detached from the ground fabric. Complete the bar with buttonhole stitches and continue the outlining.*

BUTTONHOLE STITCH

Bring the needle out on the bottom line. Insert it directly above on the top line and, making a straight stitch downwards, bring the needle out on the bottom line close to the first stitch, with the thread under the needle point. Pull up the thread to form a firm loop and repeat.

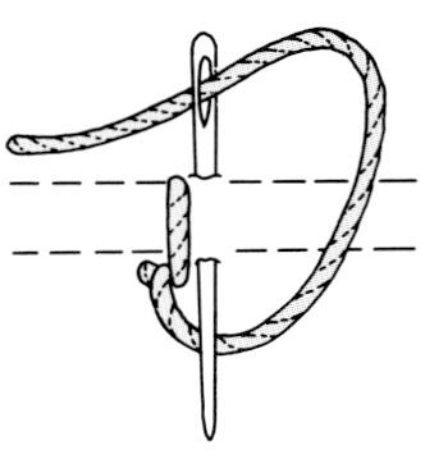

If you have never embroidered cutwork before, you could practise by tracing a single flower motif from the tablecloth and working it on a small piece of fabric, which you could use for a pin-cushion or scatter cushion. To show the cutwork off to best effect, you could place a contrast fabric underneath. Alternatively, you could try out a small corner motif on an existing table napkin, for example, or work a single flower motif in the corner of a pillow cover.

Cutwork Tablecloth

For a circular cloth measuring 228cm (90in) in diameter, you will need:

- **2.30m (1¾yd) square of white, medium-weight cotton**
- **DMC stranded embroidery cotton in the following colours: 7 skeins 3716 and 10 skeins 564**
- **No 7 crewel needle**
- **Fine-pointed embroidery scissors**
- **Tracing paper**
- **Dressmaker's carbon paper**
- **Graph pattern given on page III**

PREPARING THE FABRIC Wash and press cotton fabric to test for shrinkage. Fold the fabric in half and then into quarters. Mark the centre of the fabric both ways by basting along all four fold lines. With the fabric folded in four, place a tape measure on the centre fold and, with a pin, mark 114cm (45in) along the edge. Still holding the tape measure on the centre, move the lower end along 15cm (6in) and again place a pin at 114cm (45in) intervals. Continue in this way to the other edge. Now position more pins in between these points to complete the curve. Baste along this line through a single layer of fabric. Using a pencil, mark the cutting line 3cm (1¼ in) outside the basting stitches and cut out the cloth, cutting through all four layers. Open the fabric out and continue the line of basting around the edge.

Scale up the design from the graph pattern (see page 11), drawing straight onto tracing paper and substituting double parallel lines for the single ones of the design. Re-fold the cloth in quarters so that the basted centre lines fall in the middle of each quarter section. Pin the pattern in place, matching the centre lines and curves, and transfer it to the fabric using dressmaker's carbon paper (see page 11). Transfer the pattern to the other three quarters, open out the cloth and repeat the pattern in the spaces left to complete the border.

THE EMBROIDERY Using two strands of thread in the needle throughout, begin the embroidery by outlining the double lines in running stitch in the appropriate colours. Then, following the stitch diagrams and the stitch key, work the flower centres, embroidering the bars before the surrounding buttonhole stitch. Buttonhole the petals and larger leaves with the looped edges towards the areas to be cut away. Work the leaf veins in satin stitch (see page 13) and the smaller leaves and buds in stem stitch (see page 25).

CUTTING OUT Following the diagram given, cut away the fabric as indicated on the graph pattern. Steam press on the wrong side.

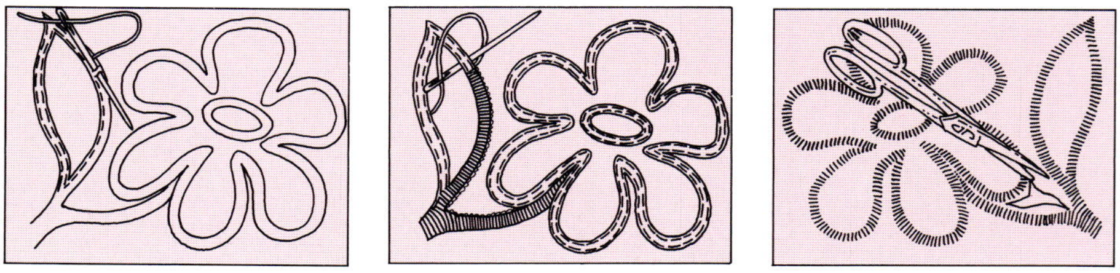

1 *Work double lines of running stitch around motif.* ***2*** *Buttonhole over stitches placing looped edge towards area to be cut away.* ***3*** *On wrong side, snip into 'cut away' areas cutting fabric close to stitching.*

This crisp white cotton cloth edged with its pretty dog rose design in pinks and greens, is evocative of leisurely meals and long summer days.

Surface Embroidery

Surface, or free-style, embroidery is one of the most popular forms of embroidery, and one that is instantly recognized by most people. It is worked on the surface of the fabric in single or mixed coloured threads, using either one stitch or any combination of stitches.

Within this category, there are several distinctive types including, for example, English Jacobean crewel embroidery, Dorset feather and Mountmellick; Chinese and Japanese embroidery (known for their beautifully shaded silk embroideries depicting naturalistic flowing designs); Indian chain stitch embroidery, and the bold colourful embroidery of Balkan traditional costumes.

The designs for surface embroidery are usually transferred to the fabric using a simple outline, and the stitching is freely worked (without counting background threads). You can transfer your own original designs by using dressmaker's carbon paper (see page 11). Alternatively, semi-transparent fabrics can be placed over the original drawing or tracing and the outline simply traced through, using a fairly hard pencil.

In choosing your fabric, bear in mind that all natural fibres are easier to embroider than synthetics, and the weight of the fabric should be neither too light nor too heavy for the type and amount of embroidery you plan to work. Medium-weight and fairly closely-woven fabrics will show off the stitching best. However, fine fabrics can always be backed with another firmer fabric to give them more weight.

For information on needles, embroidery threads and frames, see under Equipment on pages 8-9.

Stitches

The vast number of stitches used, and their variations, can be subdivided into the following groups, see the diagrams on pages 25-27.

OUTLINE STITCHES Outline stitches play a major part in all surface embroidery. As the name implies, they are used, for example, for all forms of outlining around flowers and leaves to delineate the shape; on leaves to suggest veins; in varying lengths to suggest shading and movement; for stems and other vegetation.

Included in this group are some of the easiest stitches to work, such as backstitch and stem stitch. The remaining stitches are outline, split, overcast and cable.

Stem stitch *For a single line, work from left to right along the stitch line. Keeping the thread to the left of the needle, make small, even stitches from right to left, bringing the needle out close to the previous stitch with the thread below the needle. Work infilled areas in the same way, placing the rows close together and each row following the outline shape.*

Split stitch *This is worked in a similar way to stem stitch, except that the needle emerges from the fabric a short distance back from the previous stitch, and the needle splits the thread as it is brought out of the fabric, producing an effect rather like chain stitch.*

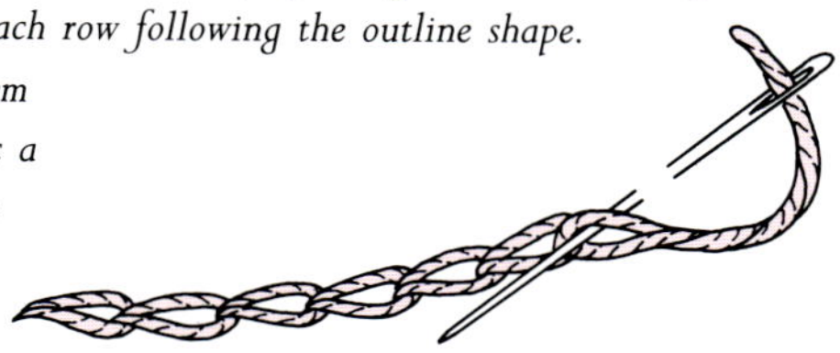

FLAT STITCHES Some of the most popular stitches are included in this group, and while stitches such as fishbone and fern stitch are relatively easy to work, others are not. A little preliminary practice is needed to get the beautiful smooth finish and sharp edges of satin stitch and flat stitch, and the subtle shading in long and short stitch. Here the diagonal threads lie close to the surface, catching and reflecting light.

Satin stitch *Bring the needle out on the stitch line and work diagonal straight stitches from bottom left to top right across the area to be filled. The stitches should lie close together and all at the same angle, and form straight edges to the embroidered shapes.*

Fern stitch *This stitch consists of three straight stitches of equal length radiating from the same central point. Bring the thread through, make a straight stitch along the line of the design, and bring the needle out at the same point. Make a similar stitch to the right and a second one to the left, and bring the needle out on the stitch line below ready to repeat the sequence.*

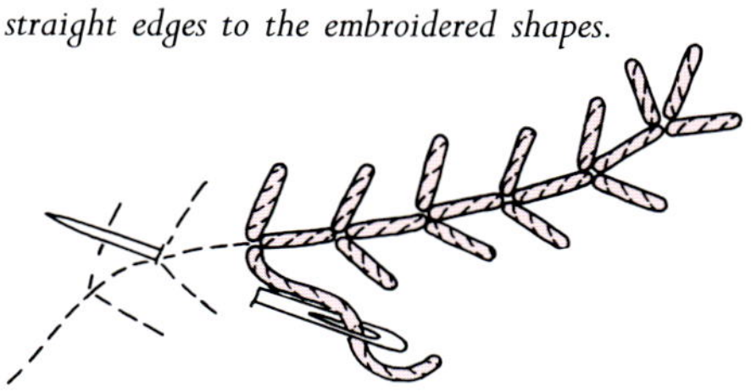

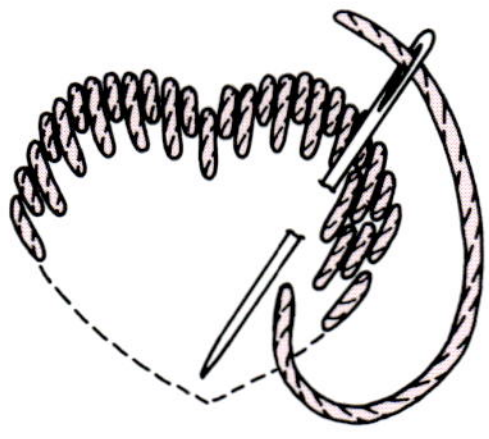

Long and short stitch *Working from the outer edge of the shape to be filled, stitch a row of alternate long and short straight stitches. Keep the outer edge even. Fill in the shape by working stitches of equal length onto the spaces left in the previous row. The irregular stitching means that colours can be graduated effectively over large areas, if needed.*

CROSSED STITCHES Refer to the chapter on Cross Stitch for information on those crossed stitches which are worked on evenweave fabric.

In addition to star stitch filling, other filling stitches – ermine stitch and St. George Cross, where the crosses are worked individually – can also be used for random spot patterns. Closed herringbone and vandyke stitch are favourites for shaping solid leaves and petals, while chevron stitch can be used effectively to make an all-over trellis pattern, and open Cretan stitch a decorative outline.

Close herringbone stitch *Working from the left, make a row of interlaced diagonal stitches by making small back stitches alternately on each side of a traced double line.*

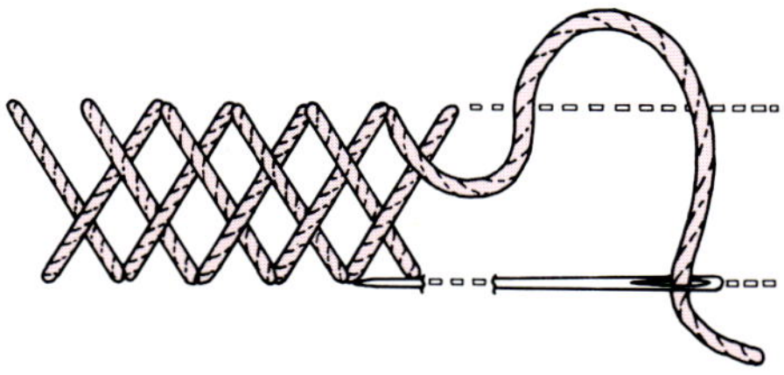

LOOPED STITCHES Many of the stitches made by looping the thread under or over the needle are fairly broad and can cover the fabric reasonably quickly. Included here is a variety of stitches ranging from braid stitches to a series of chain stitches – twisted, rosette and single – that can be used for outlining, infilling and spot patterns respectively; several types of buttonhole stitches – up and down and closed buttonhole – fly stitches, Cretan and feather stitches.

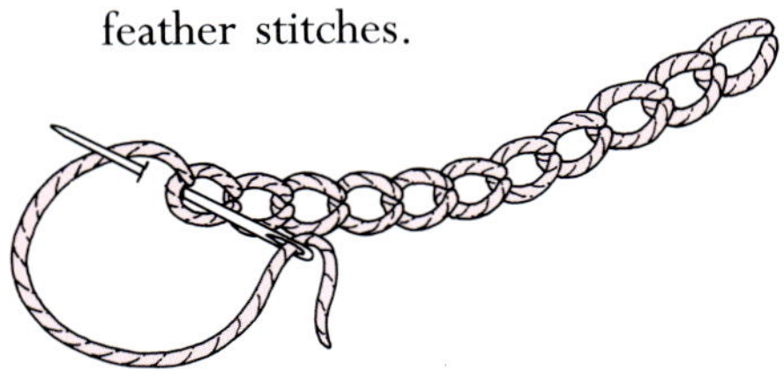

Chain stitch *Bring the thread out on the line to be worked. Holding the thread down with the left thumb, re-insert the needle at the starting point and bring it out a short distance away with the thread below the needle point, and repeat along the stitch line.*

Single chain stitch *Bring the needle out, and with the thread held down to the left, insert the needle at the starting point. Bring out a short distance away with the thread under the needle. Insert the needle under the loop to make a tying stitch, and bring it out ready to make the next stitch.*

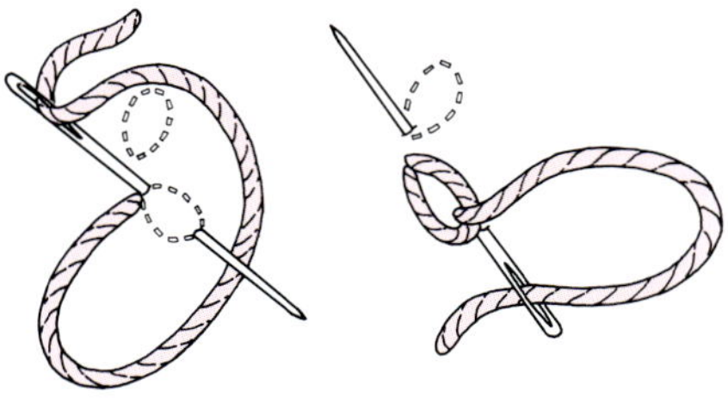

Twisted chain stitch *Begin as for ordinary chain stitch, but insert the needle close to the starting point and to the left of the thread. After making a small slanting stitch, bring the needle out on the stitch line with the thread under the point of the needle. The stitches should be worked close together for the best effect.*

Rosette chain *Working from right to left, bring the thread out on the stitch line and loop the thread to the left, holding it down with the left thumb. Make a slanting stitch from top left to borrom right bringing the needle out with the thread below. Pass the needle under the top loop without picking up any background threads, ready to make the next stitch.*

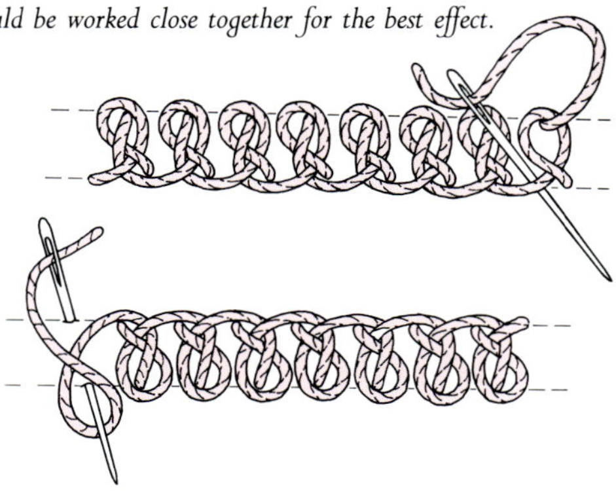

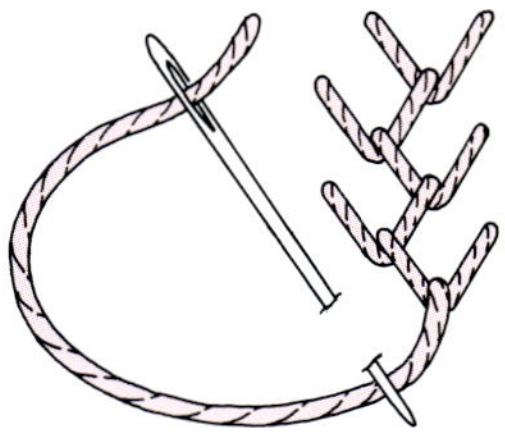

Feather stitch *Bring the thread out on the stitch line. Hold it down with the left thumb and insert the needle a short distance down to the right. Make a slanting stitch and bring the needle through on the stitch line with the thread under the needle, ready to make the next stitch in the same way.*

KNOTTED STITCHES This group of stitches offers a range of textures, from the smallest dotted effect and shaded clusters of French knots to the long twisted coils of bullion knots, and the trellis-like infilling of diamond stitch. Coral stitch and double knot are both line stitches that can be embroidered closely together to produce rich, nubbly effects.

The secret of making knots – French, bullion, four-legged cross and sword-edge stitch – is to hold the working thread firmly while the needle twists around it, and to continue holding the knot in place until the needle is passed to the back and the knot secured.

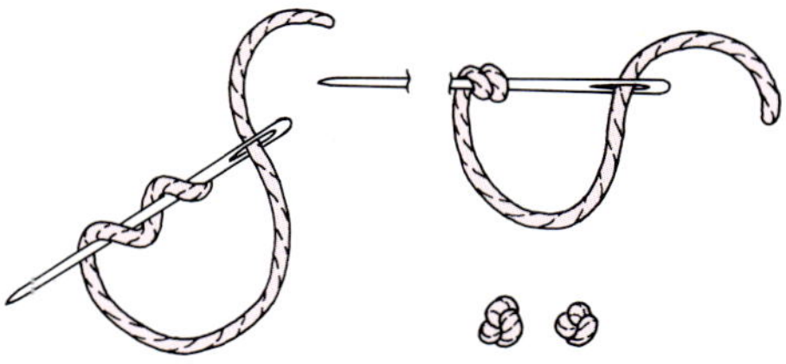

French knot *Holding the thread down with the left thumb, encircle the thread twice with the needle. Insert the needle close to the starting point and pull the needle through to the back of the embroidery before repositioning for the next stitch.*

Bullion knot *Bring the thread out, make a back stitch to the right the required size of the bullion knot, but do not pull the needle through. Twist the thread several times around the needle. Holding the coiled thread down, pull the needle through and reinsert it at the starting point, and repeat for the next stitch.*

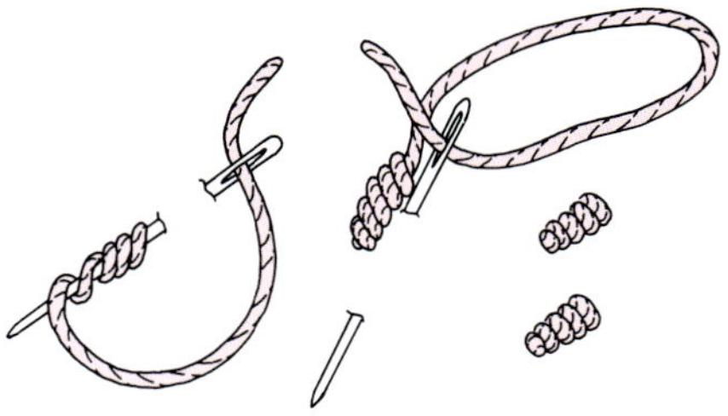

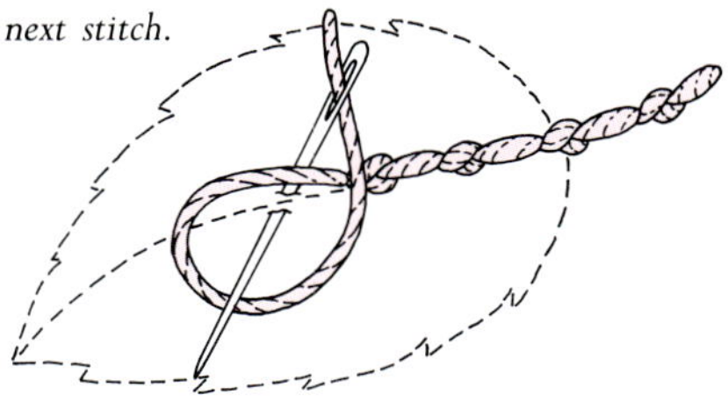

Coral stitch *Working from right to left, bring the thread through on the stitch line. Hold the thread down to the left and make a small vertical stitch across the stitch line. Bring the needle out with the thread under the needle, ready to make the next stitch.*

Double knot stitch *Working from left to right, make a small vertical stitch across the stitch line. Pass the needle downwards under the thread and pull through. Pass the needle under a second time and bring it out with the thread under the needle point. Pull the thread through to form a knot. Repeat, keeping the knots evenly spaced along the stitch line.*

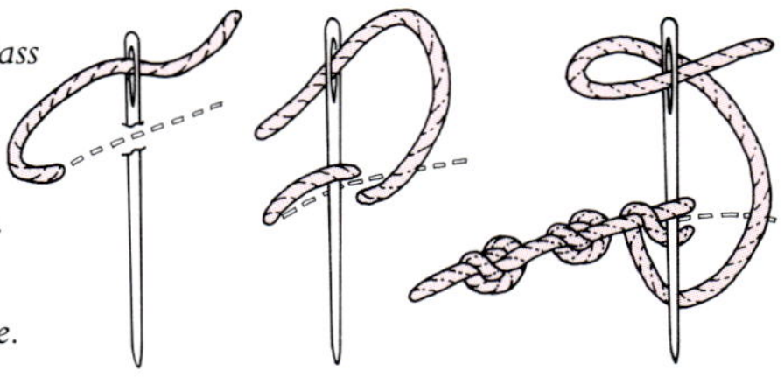

COMPOSITE STITCHES Many of the most ornamental stitch patterns with contrasting colour combinations are included in this group of stitches. They are: Pekinese stitch, whipped stem, threaded back stitch, cloud filling and guilloche, where contrasting threads are laced around a foundation of stitches. (Here a round-pointed needle is recommended for lacing threads.) Both laced herringbone and Maltese cross stitch involves some fairly complicated interlacing, so, for best results, keep the foundation stitching fairly loose.

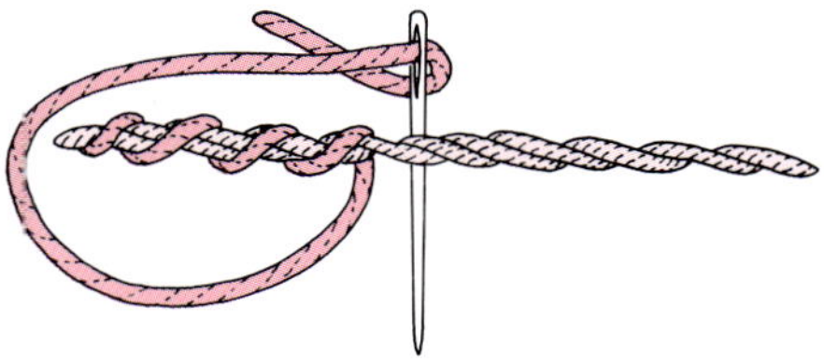

Whipped stem stitch *Work a foundation row of stem stitch first, and, with a second colour, whip over the stitches without picking up the ground fabric, as shown.*

Threaded back stitch *Work a foundation row of back stitch. Then thread through 2 contrasting colours in separate journeys without picking up ground fabric, as shown.*

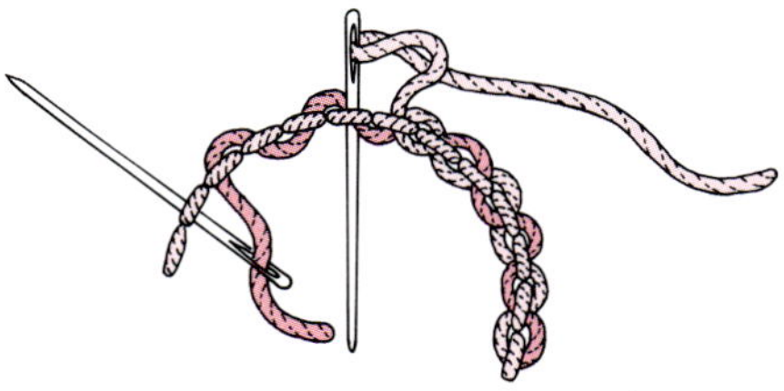

With a handful of embroidery threads and a few small pieces of fabric, you could practise some of the stitches described above – for example, mixing the stitches but using a single colour, as in Mountmellick embroidery; mixing the colours and using a single stitch, as in Dorset feather stitching, or working your own combination – there are countless permutations. You could also frame your finished sampler in a card mount, like the surface embroidered greetings cards shown on page 29.

Surfaced Embroidered Greetings Cards

For the ***Snowdrops*** card, measuring overall 20cm x 14.5cm (8in x 5¼in) with a rectangular portrait cut out, 14cm x 9.5cm (5½in x 3¾in), you will need:

- **28cm (11in) square of fine white cotton fabric (sufficient for stretching in a hoop)**
- **1 skein of white DMC (stranded embroidery cotton)**
- **No 7 crewel needle**
- **Card mount (for suppliers, see page 48)**
- **Tracing paper/carbon paper**
- **Trace pattern given on page IV**

For the ***Blackberries*** card, measuring overall 20cm x 14.5cm (8in x 5¼in) with a rectangular portrait cut out, 14cm x 9.5cm (5½in x 3¾in), you will need:

- **28cm (11in) square of unbleached calico**
- **2 skeins of 712 DMC stranded embroidery cotton**
- **No 6 crewel needle**
- **Card mount (for suppliers, see page 48)**
- **Tracing paper/carbon paper**
- **Trace pattern given on page IV**

For the ***Poppies*** card, measuring overall 20cm x 14cm (8in x 5½in) with an oval portrait cut out, 14cm x 9.5cm (5½in x 3¾in), you will need:

28cm (11in) square of fine white cotton

- **1 skein each DMC stranded embroidery cotton in the colours given with the trace pattern on page IV**
- **No 7 crewel needle**
- **Card mount (for suppliers, see page 48)**
- **Tracing paper/carbon paper**

THE EMBROIDERY For each individual card, trace the motif and transfer it to the centre of the appropriate fabric, using dressmaker's carbon paper (see page 11); and stretch in a hoop (see page 10).

What better way to personalize your greetings than to embroider and mount them yourself!

SNOWDROPS Following the stitch diagrams (pages 25-27), and using two strands of thread in the needle throughout, embroider the leaves in satin stitch, the stems in stem stitch; the bow and snowdrops in stem stitch filling, working the rows closely together and following the direction of the line, where the stitching will suggest movement and reflect light.

BLACKBERRIES Following the stitch diagrams (pages 25-27), and using four strands of thread in the needle throughout, complete the embroidery. Work the main leaves in irregular satin stitch, French knots, and the veins in a mixture of fern, feather, coral and double knot stitch; the berries in bullion knots and the flowers and sepals in satin stitch. Work the main stem in rosette chain; the tendrils in twisted chain.

POPPIES Following the stitch diagrams (pages 25-27), the colour key given with the trace pattern, and using three strands of thread in the needle for the poppies and two strands for the remaining motif, complete the embroidery. Work the poppy petals in long and short stitch, following the direction of the petals. Fill in the centre of the poppy with French knots; work the leaves and buds in satin stitch; the cornflower in single chain stitches and the stems in stem stitch.

Remove the embroidery from the hoop and steam press on the wrong side, if needed.

ASSEMBLING THE CARDS Open out the self-adhesive card mount, centre your embroidered design over the window and trim to size. Fold over the left-hand side section and press to secure.

Needlepoint

Needlepoint is one of the most popular forms of embroidery, enjoyed equally by both men and women. The wide range of canvasses and the wonderful array of yarns available, combined with all the stitches and effects that are possible, offer the needleworker great scope for creating both traditional and more innovative designs that reflect modern trends.

With a little practice, a beginner will soon discover that blocks or borders of stitches can be built up (either at random or following a pattern sequence), into very decorative geometric designs. Small stitches, such as tent stitch, half cross stitch, and so on, can be used to pick out the smallest detail in a design, or to interpret naturalistic shading in a more traditional style.

Certain needlepoint stitches have a tendency to distort the canvas – especially where they cover large areas, and if the embroidery is worked in the hand. It therefore makes sense to work the embroidery with the canvas stretched in a frame to prevent this happening. However, should a piece of needlepoint become distorted, you will need to block the finished embroidery by damp stretching.

BLOCKING AND SETTING

1 Dampen the back of the embroidery with a cloth or spray to soften the stiffening agent in the canvas, and pull gently into shape.

2 Draw the dimensions on paper with a waterproof marker and tape it to the board as a guide. Place the canvas face-down on the paper and secure with drawing pins, stretching the canvas evenly and making sure that the threads are at right angles to each other.

3 Leave to dry naturally at room temperature, when the stiffening agent will re-set as the needlepoint dries. A badly distorted canvas may need repeated settings, and perhaps a final coating of spray starch.

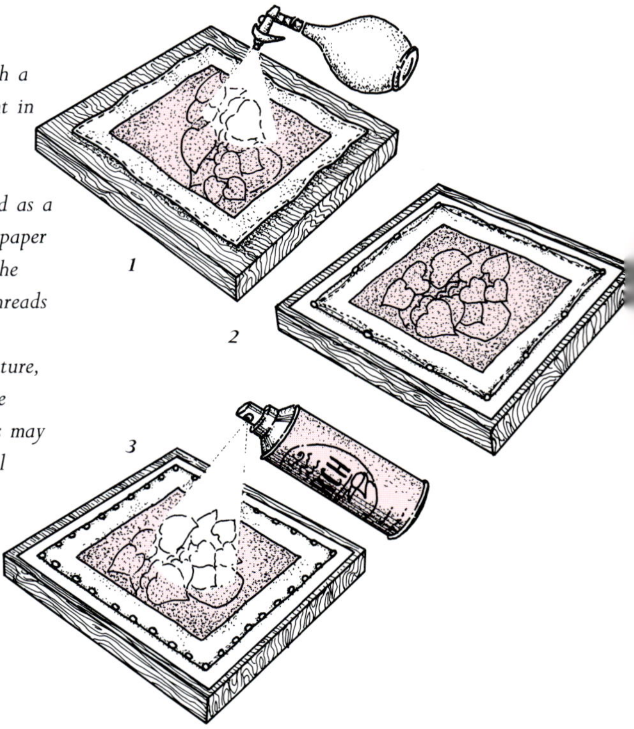

HALF CROSS STITCH This stitch looks the same as tent stitch from the right side but uses only half the amount of yarn and is therefore much more economical. However, it is less hardwearing and not recommended for chair-seat upholstery.

Bring the needle out at the top left-hand side of the area to be worked. Insert the needle diagonally upwards over a single intersection and bring it out one horizontal thread below. Work along the row, making small slanting stitches. Turn the canvas around (upside down) and work the next row in the same way; repeat in this sequence to complete the stitching. Note that the stitches on the reverse side appear vertical.

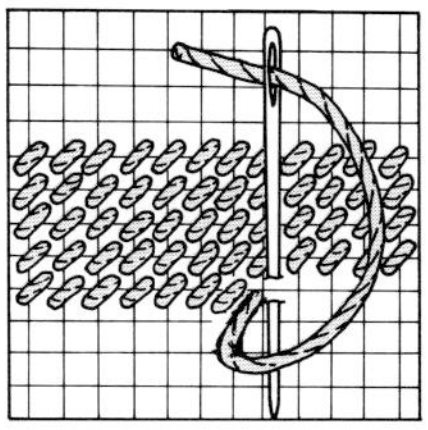

TENT STITCH Also known as petit point, tent stitch can be worked diagonally or horizontally. The diagonal method should be used whenever possible, especially over large areas, as the vertical and horizontal stitches at the back of the canvas help to prevent it from distorting.

The horizontal method is best for outlines or isolated areas of colour.

DIAGONAL TENT STITCH

1 Bring the needle through to the front of the canvas and insert it to the right of the intersection of threads above. Take the needle behind two horizontal threads so that it emerges at the bottom of the next stitch.

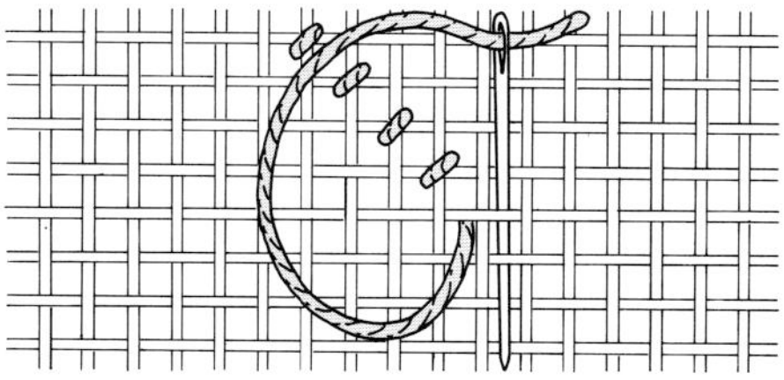

2 Work the first row from top left to bottom right and the second row from bottom right to top left. Bring the needle out at the bottom of the stitch, insert it to the right of the intersection of threads above, and take it horizontally behind two vertical threads of canvas, ready for the next stitch.

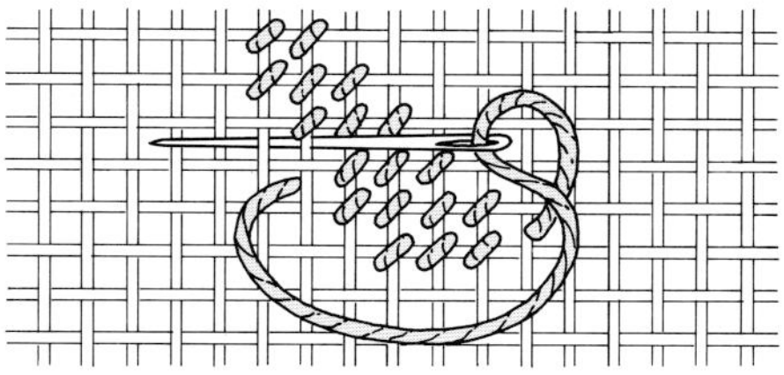

HORIZONTAL TENT STITCH *Bring the needle through to the front of the canvas and insert it to the right of the intersection of threads above. Bring the needle out below the next intersection, as shown in the diagram. Work the rows from right to left and left to right. All stitches should slant in the same direction.*

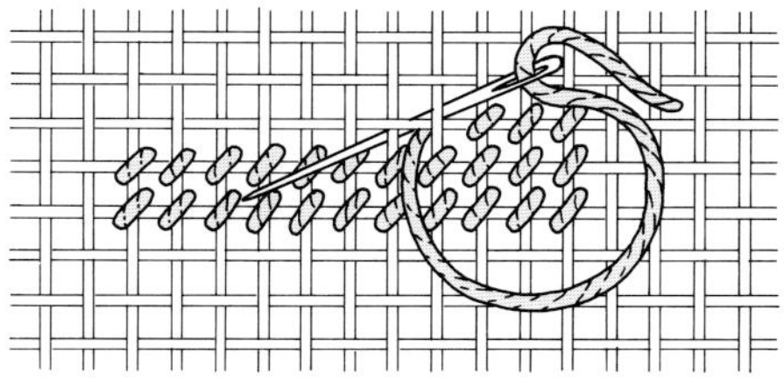

DESIGNS Designs can be charted on graph paper, where the squares are either coloured in or given a symbol with a colour key, as reference for working the embroidery. Remember when charting a design, that one square should represent one stitch – which means that, to embroider the design, you simply follow the colours given on the chart. Note, also, that in planning a design, you should always work with the measurements of your finished embroidery canvas, counting the number of squares (holes) involved and applying the same number to your graph paper. This way, you will maintain the correct finished size, even though the squares on the graph paper may not actually be the same size as the squares of the canvas mesh.

Needlepoint embroidery makes an extremely hardwearing fabric and is used for chair seating, cushions, bags, rugs, pictures and many other items.

Following the above stitch diagrams, you could practise embroidering a small sampler with blocks or bands of different colours and, possibly, trying out a variety of yarns as an introduction to needlepoint. To make a needlepoint pincushion with either a geometric or floral design, (see page 32).

NEEDLEPOINT PINCUSHIONS

For the *'Kelim'* pincushion, measuring 14cm (5½in) square, you will need:

- **20cm (8in) square of antique single canvas, 14 threads to 2.5cm (1in)**
- **17cm (6½in) square of deep yellow coarse linen backing fabric**
- **1 skein each DMC tapestry yarn in the colours given with the chart on page V**
- **No 20 tapestry needle**
- **Matching sewing threads**
- **Sufficient loose wadding for filling**

For the *'Primulas'* pincushion, measuring 11.5cm (4½in) across, you will need:

- **23cm (9in) square of white single canvas, 14 threads to 2.5cm (1in)**
- **1 skein each DMC tapestry yarn in the colours given with the chart on page V**
- **No 20 tapestry needle**
- **Pincushion mould with wooden surround, measuring 11.5cm (4½in) in diameter.**

THE EMBROIDERY Work both pincushions in the following way. With small pieces of canvas, such as these pincushions, first mark the centre both ways with basting stitches, and then either machine stitch strips of strong cotton fabric around each edge and stretch in a large hoop or in a small rectangular frame, in the usual way. Alternatively, the canvas can be secured by the strips of fabric to a canvas stretcher or to the back of an unwanted picture frame, using drawing pins.

These charming pincushions would make most acceptable gifts for very special friends. The sewing pins could always be substituted for your favourite brooches and other jewelry.

Following the appropriate chart and stitch diagram, complete the embroidery. Half cross stitch uses the least yarn and is quite suitable for pincushions.

In the case of the Primulas design, use two strands of yarn throughout, embroidering the design first and then the background. Remove from the frame and take out the basting stitches.

MAKING UP THE PINCUSHIONS For the Kelim cushion, place the backing and embroidery right sides together, and then pin and baste around the edge, stitching close to the border. Trim the seam allowance to 1cm (3/8in). Machine stitch around, leaving an 8cm (3in) opening in one side. Remove the basting stitches. Turn right side out and insert the filling. Slip stitch the opening to close.

For the Primulas cushion, lay the embroidery face-down and cut out of canvas allowing about 2.5cm (1in) beyond the background stitching. Using strong thread, run gathering stitches just outside the embroidery; centre the embroidery over the mould and pin to hold. Pull up the gathering thread, even out the gathers on the underside of the mould, and secure the thread firmly. Attach the mould to the base with the screw provided.

CHAPTER
SEVEN

Hand-Sewn Quilting

With the exception of the purely decorative forms of quilting (Italian Trapunto and Corded), quilting involves stitching together two layers of fabric enclosing a soft filling material. Tied or Tufted quilting is the simplest, in which strands of thread are taken twice through the three layers of fabric and tied in a double knot, the knots being spaced at regular intervals over the entire surface.

Wadded quilting is the traditional English method and has a soft layer of wadding inserted between two outer layers which are held in place by small stitches decoratively worked over the entire surface – traditionally by hand. Closely woven fabrics such as cotton, cotton/wool mix, silk and sateen are ideal for the top layer. Choose muslin or lawn for the bottom layer for items like cushion covers, but for reversible bed quilts, either the same fabric or a slightly firmer one is recommended for the bottom layer, so that the puffiness of the quilting will be thrown forward.

Washable synthetic wadding is mainly used between the two layers (see page 7). Cotton wadding, wool and domette are available, but items made using the two latter fillings will need to be dry-cleaned.

Quilting Designs

Historically, wadded quilting developed as a practical means of stitching together layers of fabric to produce the much-loved patchwork quilt. In Britain regional traditions of quilting developed in Durham, Cumberland, Northumberland, Westmorland, Wales and South West England. Such quilts today are highly prized and are collectors' pieces.

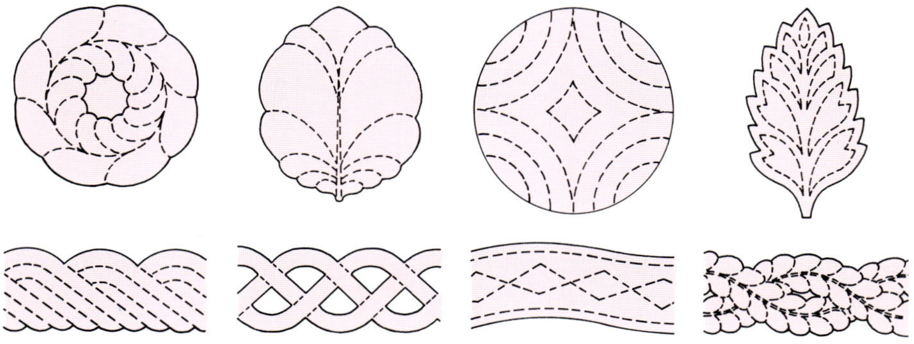

The designs, however, can still be reproduced, and provide a fascinating insight into the history of quilting. Typical traditional quilting patterns include spirals, leaves, hearts, roses, lovers' knots, fans, feathers, shells and chains. Many of these motifs can be bought as trace patterns and quilting stencils from craft suppliers. Old quilt designs are mainly composed of single images placed around a prominent central motif linked with background 'filler' patterns, and are bordered and decorated with distinctive corner motifs.

In contrast, modern quilting often follows a more relaxed style and the designs can range from freely-drawn figurative compositions to all-over random quilting, and individual motifs outlined with simple contour quilting.

Cutting and Marking the Fabric

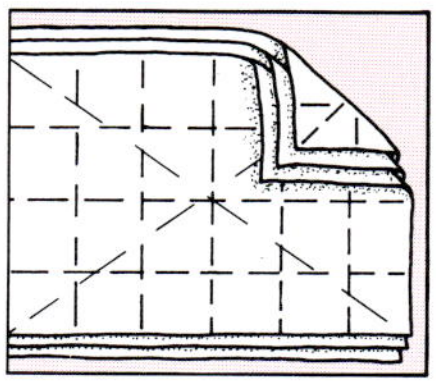

Cut the 3 layers of fabric (top, wadding and backing) slightly larger than the finished size. Mark the design on the right side of the top fabric before assembling the layers.

Marking can be done in several ways: for drawing around a stencil or template, use one of the following pencils: a sharp-pointed 2H lead, coloured or silver. Dressmaker's water-erasable pencils are also available and are very popular with many craft workers. The traditional method is to score the outline using a round-ended needle, with the fabric placed on a padded surface to ensure a well-scored line. Trace patterns can be transferred using carbon paper, but remember to choose a light colour for dark fabrics and a close tone for other coloured fabrics. This will prevent the excess carbon in strong colours from staining the quilting threads.

PREPARING TO QUILT Although wadded quilting can be worked in the hand, a quilting hoop or frame is recommended. This keeps the layers together and evenly stretched. A quilting hoop can be used for large items by moving it along after completing a section. For full size quilts, a quilting frame is recommended.

USING A HOOP Begin by assembling the layers and baste them in both directions, first diagonally through the centre and then in rows about 6cm (2½in) apart. Avoid knots by working outwards from the middle, leaving half the thread length when basting one half row, and returning to re-thread and complete the row in the opposite direction.

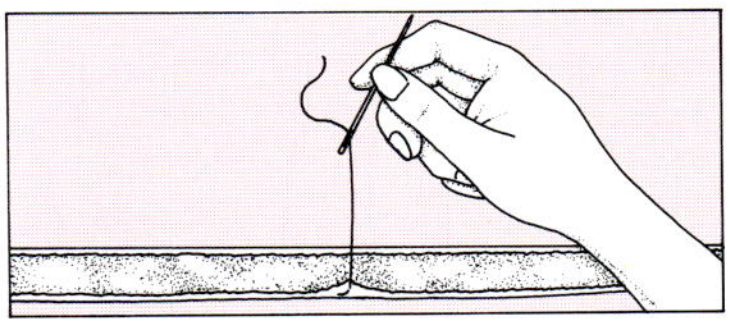

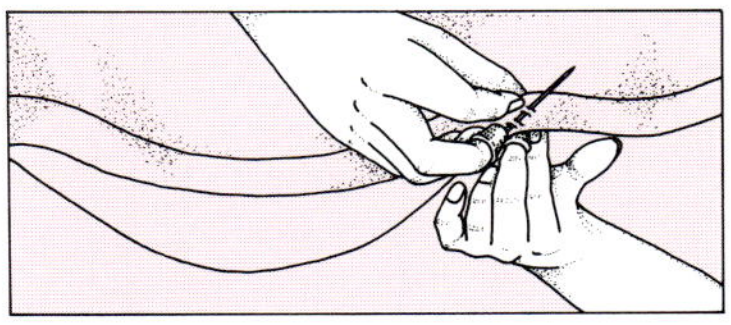

With the fabric stretched evenly in the hoop, thread a quilting needle with a short length of quilting thread and knot the end. Beginning at the centre of the design, pull the knot through the backing into the wadding and work small, evenly-spaced running stitches around the design, stitching through all layers. Keep one hand underneath the work and wear a thimble on that hand to push the needle back through the fabric. For quilting close to the edges, attach strips of fabric around the work, so that the edges can be stretched within the hoop.

Feather Circle Cushion Cover

For a cushion, measuring 41cm (16in) square, you will need:

- **Two pieces 46cm (18in) square of off-white cotton sateen 46cm (18in) square lightweight synthetic wadding 46cm (18in) square of white muslin**
- **2 skeins of Anchor coton à broder No8, colour 62**
- **No 7 crewel needle**
- **1.70m (2yd) No3 piping cord**
- **Matching sewing threads**
- **Tracing paper**
- **43cm (17in) square cushion pad**
- **Trace pattern given on page III**

THE QUILTING The diagram gives a quarter section of the design which should first be enlarged to size, working directly on to tracing paper, see page 11. Alternatively, use a photocopying machine to increase the design to 18.5cm (7¼in) square.

Transfer it to one of the pieces of top fabric, using dressmaker's carbon paper in a closely matched colour, so that it will not show too strongly, see page 11. Reverse the tracing on the centre lines to complete the design.

Prepare the layers as for wadded quilting and follow the instructions given for working in a hoop. Using simple running stitch, quilt the design, working outwards from the centre. Remove the finished quilting from the hoop. Trim the edges to size, allowing for 1cm (⅜in) seam allowances all round.

MAKING UP THE CUSHION Remove the basting stitches. Place the top and the cushion backing fabrics right sides together and trim the backing to size. Baste and machine stitch contrast piping around the edges of the top layer, right sides together.

With both the top and backing pieces right sides together, baste and machine stitch around, taking 1cm (⅜in) seams and leaving a 25cm (10in) opening in one side. Neaten the seams by overcasting, snip into the corners, and turn through to the right side. Insert the cushion pad and, using matching sewing thread, slip stitch the opening to close.

Contour-Quilted Cushion

For a cushion, measuring 38cm (15in) square, you will need:

- **50cm (½yd) of printed floral cotton, 122cm (48in) wide (includes sufficient fabric for bias-cut piping) 46cm (18in) square of contrast cotton for the cushion backing 46cm (18in) square of lightweight synthetic wadding 46cm (18in) square of white muslin**
- **Quilting threads or sewing threads in colours to match the printed design**
- **No 8 betweens needle**
- **Matching sewing threads**
- **1.50m (1¾yd) No5 piping cord**
- **41cm (16in) square cushion pad**
- **Tracing paper**

PREPARING THE DESIGN Before cutting out a 46cm (18in) square from the main fabric, decide which part of the motif would be best in the centre of the

cushion. Cut out the top layer to size, putting the remaining fabric to one side for the piping.

Working on a firm surface, smooth out the fabric and place the tracing paper on top. Outline the main areas (islands) you wish to quilt around. Draw echoing lines around them, about 12mm (½ in) apart. Continue in this way until the outer points of the islands almost converge. Then fill in the areas left with similar lines, adjusting them, if needed, until they make a pleasing balance.

QUILTING AND MAKING UP THE CUSHION Prepare and quilt the fabric, following the instructions given for the Feather Circle cushion cover. Using your traced design as a guide, quilt the outline of the central motifs in matching threads. Then, working freehand, draw in the next contour outline around each island and quilt in one of the colours in the print. Referring to your traced design, complete the quilting. Make up the cushion cover, following the instructions given for the Feather Circle cushion cover.

Cushions showing contrasting styles of quilting on plain and patterned fabrics.

Block Patchwork

Patchwork involves cutting fabric into different sizes and shapes and stitching them together to make an entirely new fabric. the construction methods can be divided into all–over mosaic designs or 'block' patterns. A block is a complete pattern, usually square and made up of smaller geometric shapes. The completed blocks are then stitched together to make the finished patchwork. Patterns can easily be extended or reduced to fit specific requirements. Lattice strips (borders) can be added between blocks and the entire patchwork bordered with plain, patterned or patched fabric.

Alternatively, strips of fabric can be applied to a backing fabric to form the block, as in Log cabin (or Canadian) patchwork. This is a well-known American design where each block is composed of contrasting light and dark strips of fabric placed around a central square. The arrangement of the strips is said to represent the logs of the log cabins built by early American settlers.

The central square represents the fire, or hearth, and is traditionally red. The light-coloured strips on one side of the block suggest light within the cabin, and the dark strips the shadows.

Fabrics

The advantage of this design is that all kinds of left-over scraps can be utilized. Medium-weight fabrics that take a crease well are generally suitable. Both prints and plain colours may be used, although prints should be small-scale, and it is customary to use a plain colour for the centre square. If you wish to create a light/dark pattern, you should buy equal amounts of fabric in the two contrasting colour ranges.

You will also need backing fabric for the blocks. This could be lightweight interfacing, calico or muslin, depending on the desired effect.

Making The Block

The following steps show how to construct a block, the finished size measuring approximately 25cm (10in) square with 2.5cm (1in) wide strips and a 5cm (2in) central square. Smaller blocks can be made, simply by applying fewer strips or by using narrower strips.

1 *Cut a square of backing fabric to size plus 15mm (1/2in) seam allowances all round. Mark it diagonally both ways, either by basting stitches or with a light pencil line.*

2 *Pin a 5cm (2in) square in the centre and secure it with small running stitches (or use machine stitching).*

3 *Cut a light strip 6mm (1/4in) longer at each end than the central square, by 4cm (1 1/2in) wide. With right sides together, and the raw edges matching, stitch across.*

4 *Press the strip back to the right side. Apply a second light strip 6mm (1/4in) longer at each end than the length of the central square and strip; stitch and press back.*

5 *Apply dark strips in the same way, working around the square, Stitching and pressing them back to the right side.*

6 *Repeat the sequence, adding light and dark strips to complete the block.*

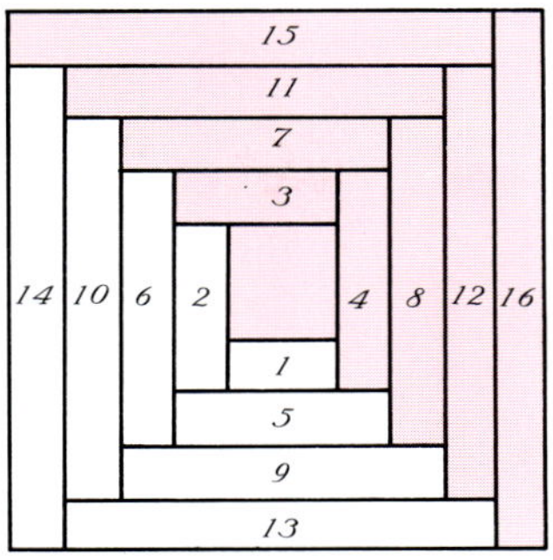

1

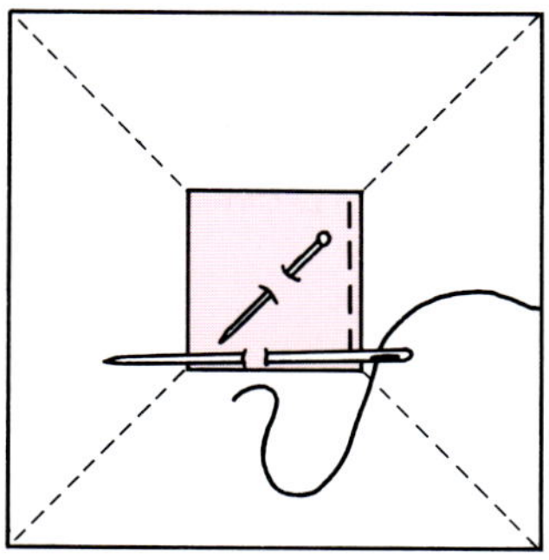
2

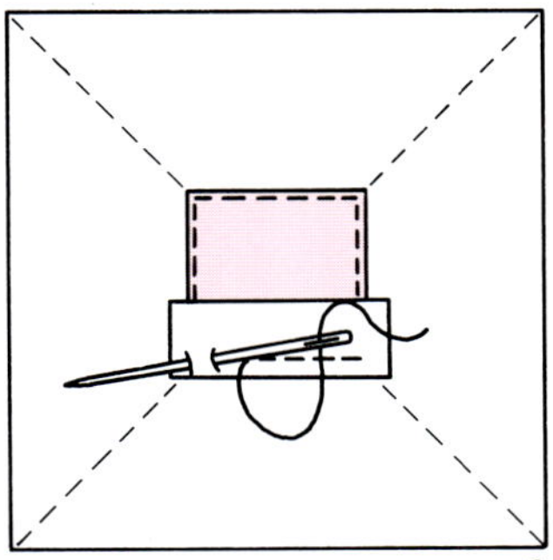
3

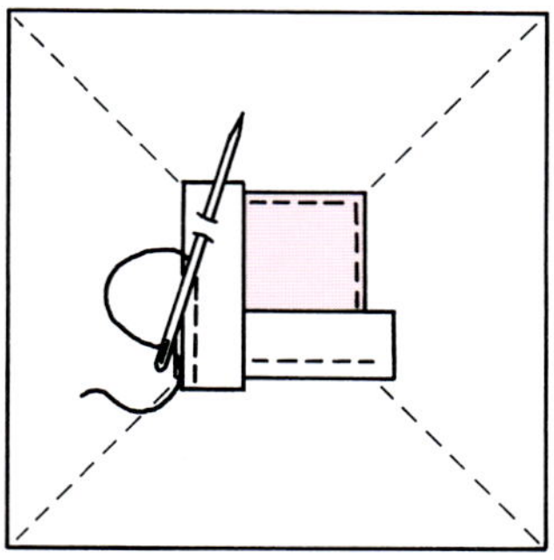
4

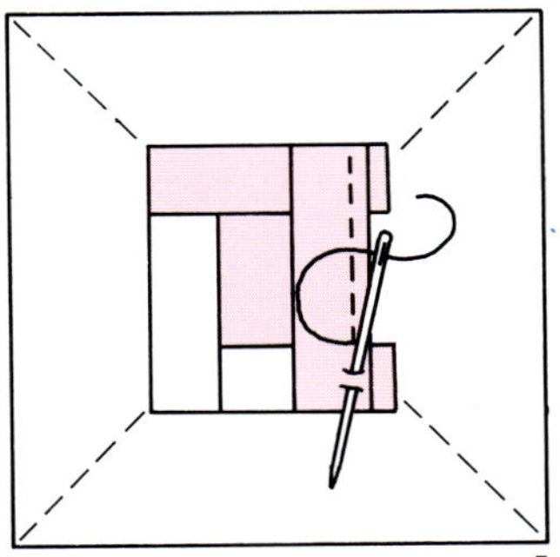
5

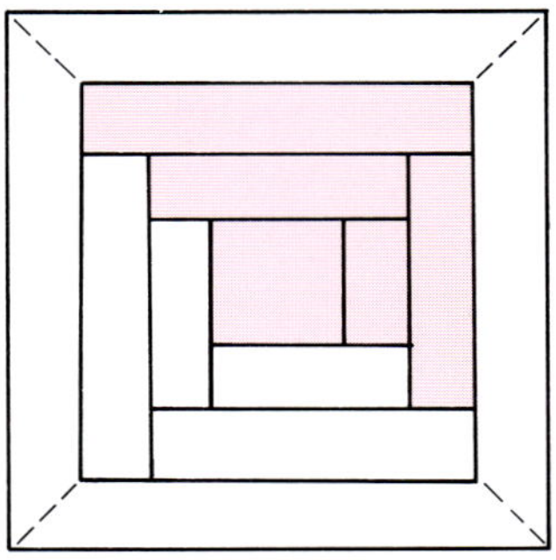
6

FINISHING *The patchwork is not always bordered but it should be lined and top-stitched between the seams of the blocks, or tied at strategic points.*

For making full-size quilts, a 30cm (12in) square block is popular and for cushions or smaller items, a 15cm (6in) square block is usual.

TYING THE PATCHWORK Evenly-spaced knots at 15cm (6in) intervals make a neat alternative to quilting, especially where very thick wadding is used.

For the knot, make a loose double stitch through all layers, leaving a long end on top. Tie both ends firmly with a reef knot. Trim and leave the ends on either side of the work.

Note: on full-size quilts, use a thick cotton thread and a long (chenille) needle for making the knots.

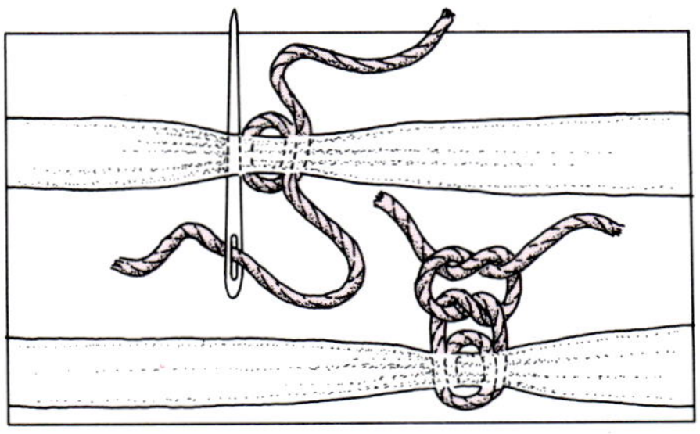

Doll's Crib Quilt in Log Cabin Patchwork

For a quilt, measuring 42cm x 27cm (16½in x 10½in), you will need:

- **4 different, light-coloured cotton fabrics (plain pinks and yellows)**
- **4 different, dark-coloured cotton fabrics (plain greys and greens),**
- **90cm (36in) wide: 15cm (6in) of each for the strips**
- **45cm (18in) of (red) for the centre squares and for the quilt lining, including the border**
- **42cm x 27cm (16½in x 10½in) of lightweight synthetic wadding**
- **45cm (18in) square (approximately) of unbleached calico, for backing the blocks**

THE LOG CABIN PATCHWORK Following the diagrams given for the two blocks, cut sufficient strips of fabric, adding 6mm (¼in) seam allowances all round. From the calico, cut out fifteen 10cm (4in) squares. Applying the strips as shown, complete the blocks.

Lay out the blocks in pattern, following the positioning diagram: rows A and B. Taking 12mm (½in) seams, pin, baste and stitch the blocks together, to make five horizontal rows. Trim the seams and press open. Then join the rows together, trim and press the seams open. The patchwork should measure 23cm x 38cm (9in x 15in).

Cut the red backing fabric to measure 47cm x 32cm (18in x 12½in). Lay it on a clean surface, right-side down. Place the wadding and the patchwork centrally on top, right-side up. Smooth out and baste the layers together, working from the centre out. Either hand quilt the layers together, stitching between the blocks, or tie the layers at the corners of each block using two strands of green sewing thread (see the diagram on page 39).

Make a 6mm(¼in) turning on the backing fabric and fold it over the raw edges of the quilt top to form a 2cm (¾in) border, turning in the two long edges first and finishing with the two short edges. Pin, baste and, using matching sewing thread, slip stitch in place. Remove the basting stitches.

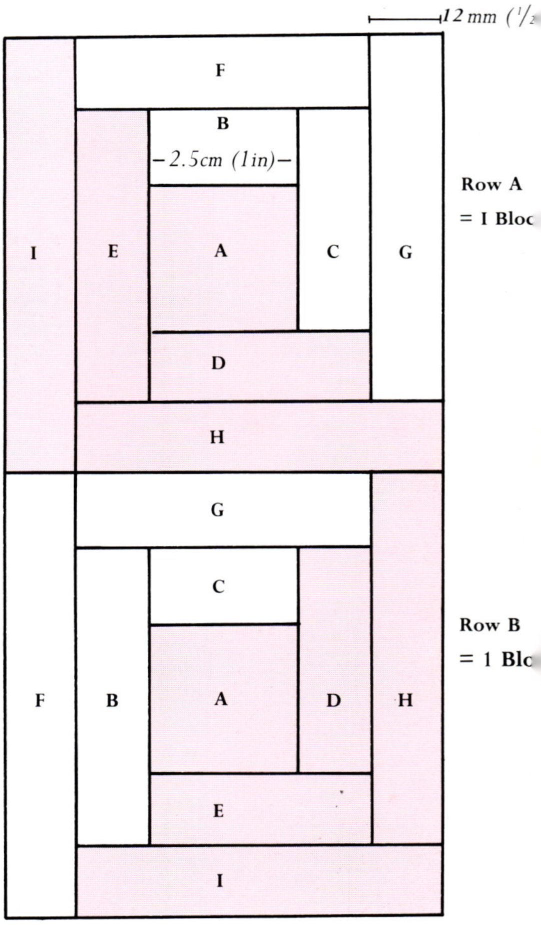

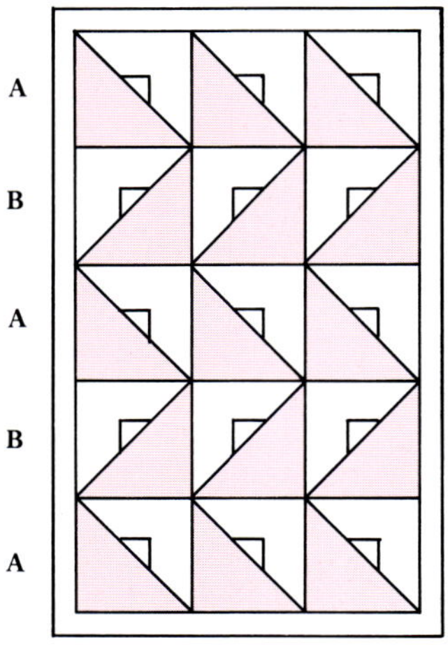

positioning diagram

Fabric Colour Key
A Red
B Pale Yellow
C Yellow
D Green
E Grey
F Pale Pink
G Pink
H Dark Grey Green
I Dark Green

A colourful quilt to delight any child — either in these colours or those of your choice.

CHAPTER
•NINE•

Picture Appliqué

Appliqué is the process whereby fabric shapes are cut out and applied to a foundation fabric, usually by means of stitching, although adhesives are used for picture appliqué where laundering does not need to be considered. The stitching can be either plain or decoratively embroidered, hand- or machine-stitched.

Unlike more practical forms of appliqué, where matching fabric weights and turnings have to be considered, picture appliqué is unrestricted – indeed, it can be a vital art form in which personal statements are expressed. The play of light on surfaces, the juxtaposition of fabrics used to create subtle modelling, the choice of stitchery and colours, may all be exploited to create pieces of appliqué with immense tactile qualities.

Fabrics

In selecting the most appropriate fabrics to interpret a picture, such as the house picture shown on page 45, bear in mind that prints should be small-scale, for curtains and flower blossoms, for example. Fine tweeds and slub linens are useful for bricks and stonework; small geometric patterns for tiles (Victorian garden path); lace for curtains; muslin for clouds; fine, plain cottons for sky; piqué cottons to suggest vertical cladding or panelling; two-tone chambray or linen for gravel (roads), and so on. One of the most exciting features of picture appliqué is making fabric 'work', not just in colour and shape but in pattern and texture. Patterned fabrics can be used to suggest all kinds of images – stripes for ploughed fields, flower sprigs for blossom, pile surfaces for animal fur, and small checks for brickwork.

For picture-making, a lightweight, iron-on interfacing is applied to the back of the fabric before the shape is cut out, to avoid having to make turnings, and to prevent the edges from fraying.

DESIGNS For a 'house' picture, it is best to start with a preliminary drawing from a colour photograph of your house. This helps to simplify the images into areas of colour and texture before selecting the fabrics.

Begin by enlarging the photograph to size; most photocopying services can do this fairly instantly, otherwise follow the instructions on page 11.

After making a simplified drawing of your house picture, visualise which fabrics will need to be applied first, and then number the areas in that order. Repeat the number where several pieces are applied at the same stage, such as the clouds and window frames in the picture illustrated above.

Number the individual areas of your drawing in the order the fabrics will be applied, starting with those farthest away, such as sky and distant fields, for example. Make a tracing of the complete picture, and then, using dress-maker's carbon paper, transfer it to the right-side of the ground fabric, following the straight grain. Similarly, transfer the outline of each section separately onto a second sheet of paper; note which edges will overlap others and which will need extending, and cut them out to use as templates. Mark the straight grain on each one, and number them in order of application.

STITCHING It is not essential to stitch every piece of applied fabric, particularly where several layers are built up, or when shapes are very small, such as the leaves on the house picture project: they can be stuck down using PVA wood glue. This is recommended in preference to fabric adhesive which, because of its rubbery consistency, cannot be stitched through.

Machine stitching is most suitable for picture appliqué whereas hand stitching is used most effectively for adding surface details, such as the pampas grass on the project. Sewing threads and embroidery threads in varying thicknesses can be used, depending on the desired effect.

'My House' Picture in Appliqué

For a picture, measuring 22cm x 17cm (8½in x 6½in), you will need:

- **28cm x 23cm (11in x 9in) of unbleached calico (includes 6cm (2½in) extra fabric all round for stretching the finished picture over card)**
- **A selection of fabrics (measuring not more than 20cm x 15cm (8in x 6in)**
- **Blue cotton for sky; white muslin for clouds; brown tweeds for house and walls; floral prints for curtains and flower garden; white cotton for paint trim; yellow cotton for door and fence; white ribbons for window trims, 1.5mm (⅛in) and 3mm (1/10in) wide; slub linen for footpath; mixed satins and wool for green creeper; yellow stranded embroidery thread for pampas grass**
- **Matching sewing threads**
- **22cm x 17cm (8½in x 6½in) of stiff card for mounting the appliqué**
- **PVA wood glue**
- **38cm (15in) square of lightweight, iron-on interfacing**
- **Picture frame of your choice**

THE APPLIQUÉ Enlarge the design to size and transfer the main outline to the background calico. Apply the iron-on interfacing and cut out the appliqué patches, allowing extra fabric on underlapping edges (those fabrics which are behind others in perspective. Position them in the correct order and, working in the hand, stitch them in place, or use adhesive where appropriate. In the house picture, the following edges are machine-stitched, using zigzag stitch throughout set at 1½ stitches wide by 1 stitch long: the clouds, curtains, door, fanlight and surrounding paint trim, fences, garden wall and flower bed. All other patches are stuck down.

Using embroidery thread, work straight stitches to suggest the pampas grass. On a scrap of calico, hand-paint the family pet cat using two tones of brown, and black whiskers; cut out and glue in place.

Stretch the finished appliqué over the cardboard, lacing it across the back, see page 11 ready for putting it in the picture frame.

Protectively framed under glass, an appliquéd house picture would make an ideal gift to celebrate a wedding anniversary.

BUTTERFLIES
AND OTHER INSECTS OF BRITAIN

This delightful collection of projects, showing a variety of needlecrafts, includes some which are eminently suitable for beginners, such as the lavender sachets, as well as others that are a little more challenging.

Acknowledgements

The author would like to thank the following people who helped in making the projects for the book with such skill and enthusiasm: Sheila Coulson, Caroline Davies, Christina Eustace, Janet Grey, Wendy Milloy, Jennifer Nash and Hilda Vesma.

Supplier

the following mail order company will supply those particular items mentioned in the list of requirements for making the projects in this book.

Framecraft Miniatures Limited
148-150 High Street
Aston
Birmingham B6 4US
Telephone (021) 359 4442

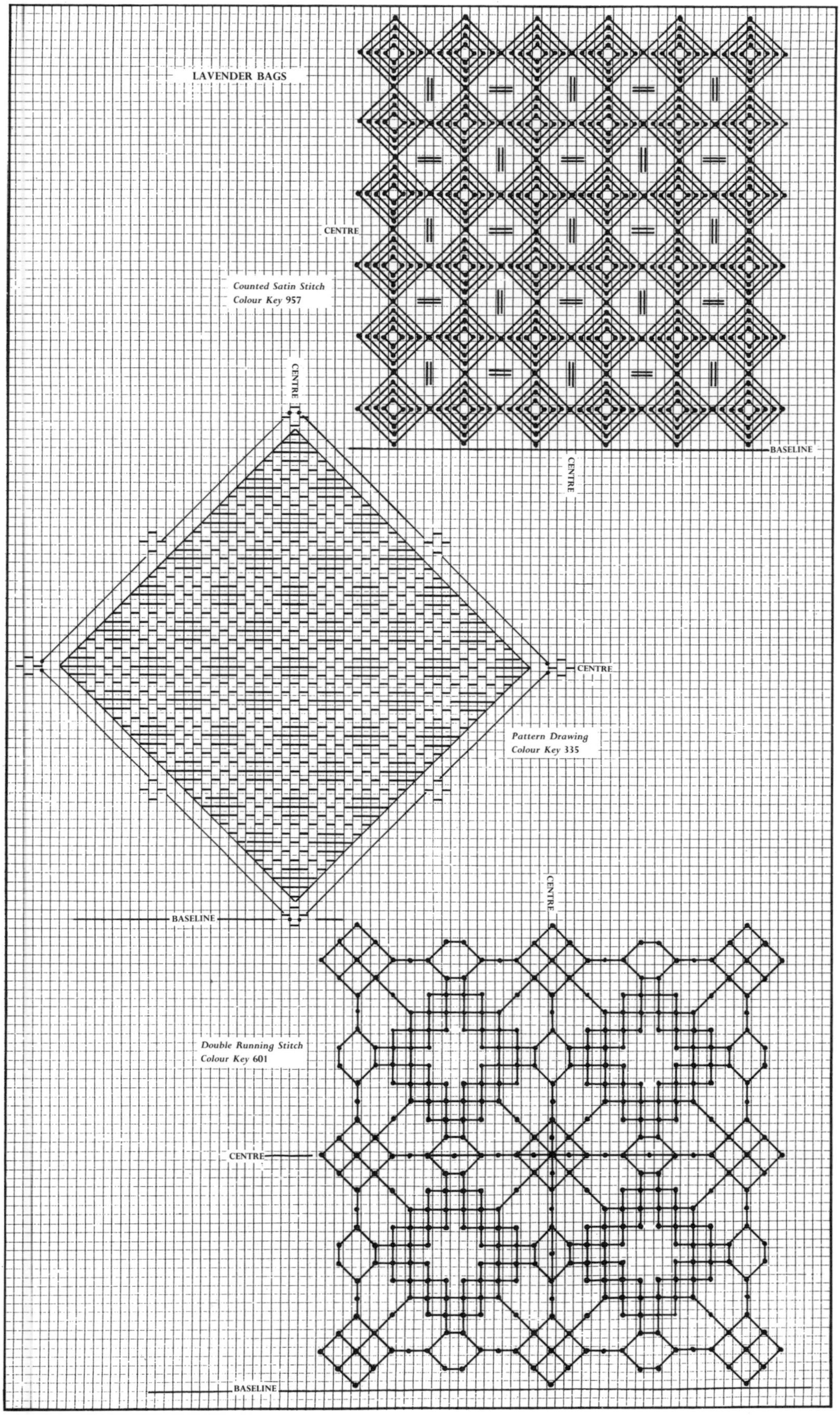
LAVENDER BAGS
CENTRE
Counted Satin Stitch
Colour Key 957
CENTRE
BASELINE
CENTRE
CENTRE
Pattern Drawing
Colour Key 335
BASELINE
CENTRE
Double Running Stitch
Colour Key 601
CENTRE
BASELINE

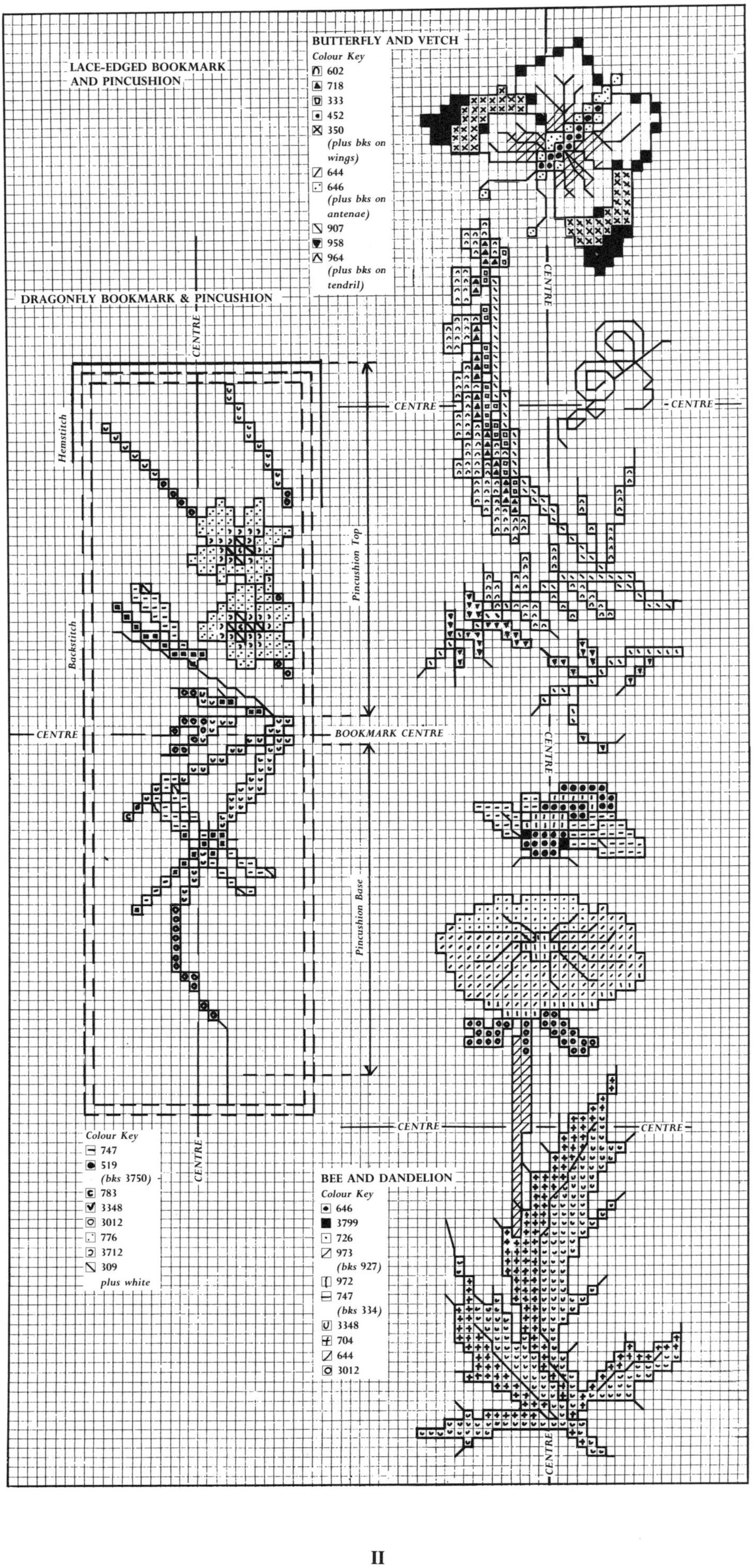
LACE-EDGED BOOKMARK AND PINCUSHION
BUTTERFLY AND VETCH
Colour Key
602
718
333
452
350
(plus bks on wings)
644
646
(plus bks on antenae)
907
958
964
(plus bks on tendril)
DRAGONFLY BOOKMARK & PINCUSHION
CENTRE
Hemstitch
Backstitch
Pincushion Top
BOOKMARK CENTRE
Pincushion Base
Colour Key
747
519
(bks 3750)
783
3348
3012
776
3712
309
plus white
BEE AND DANDELION
Colour Key
646
3799
726
973
(bks 927)
972
747
(bks 334)
3348
704
644
3012

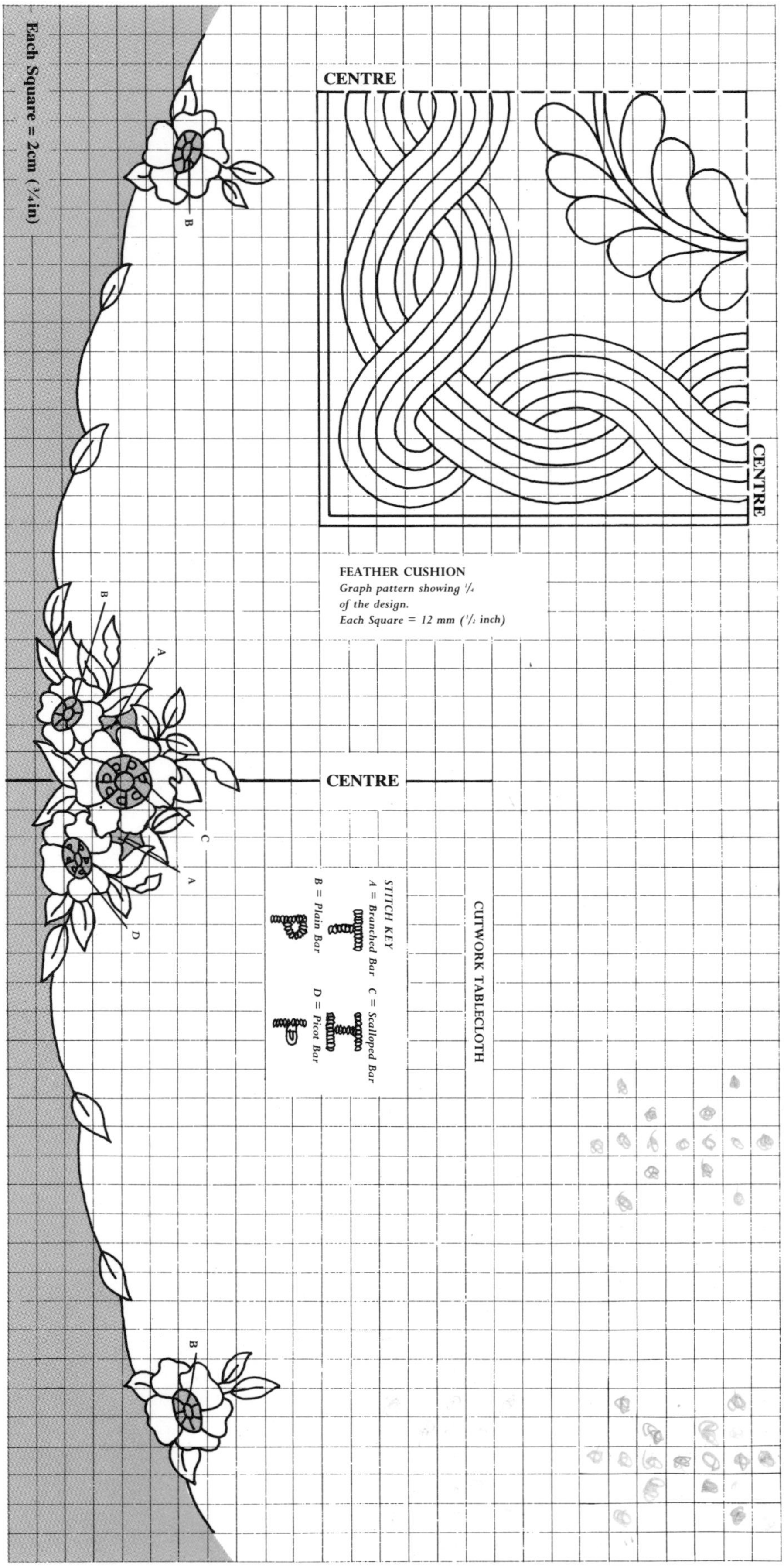
Each Square = 2cm (3/4in)
CENTRE
CENTRE
FEATHER CUSHION
Graph pattern showing 1/4 of the design.
Each Square = 12 mm (1/2 inch)
CENTRE
CUTWORK TABLECLOTH
STITCH KEY
A = Branched Bar C = Scalloped Bar
B = Plain Bar D = Picot Bar
A
B
C
D

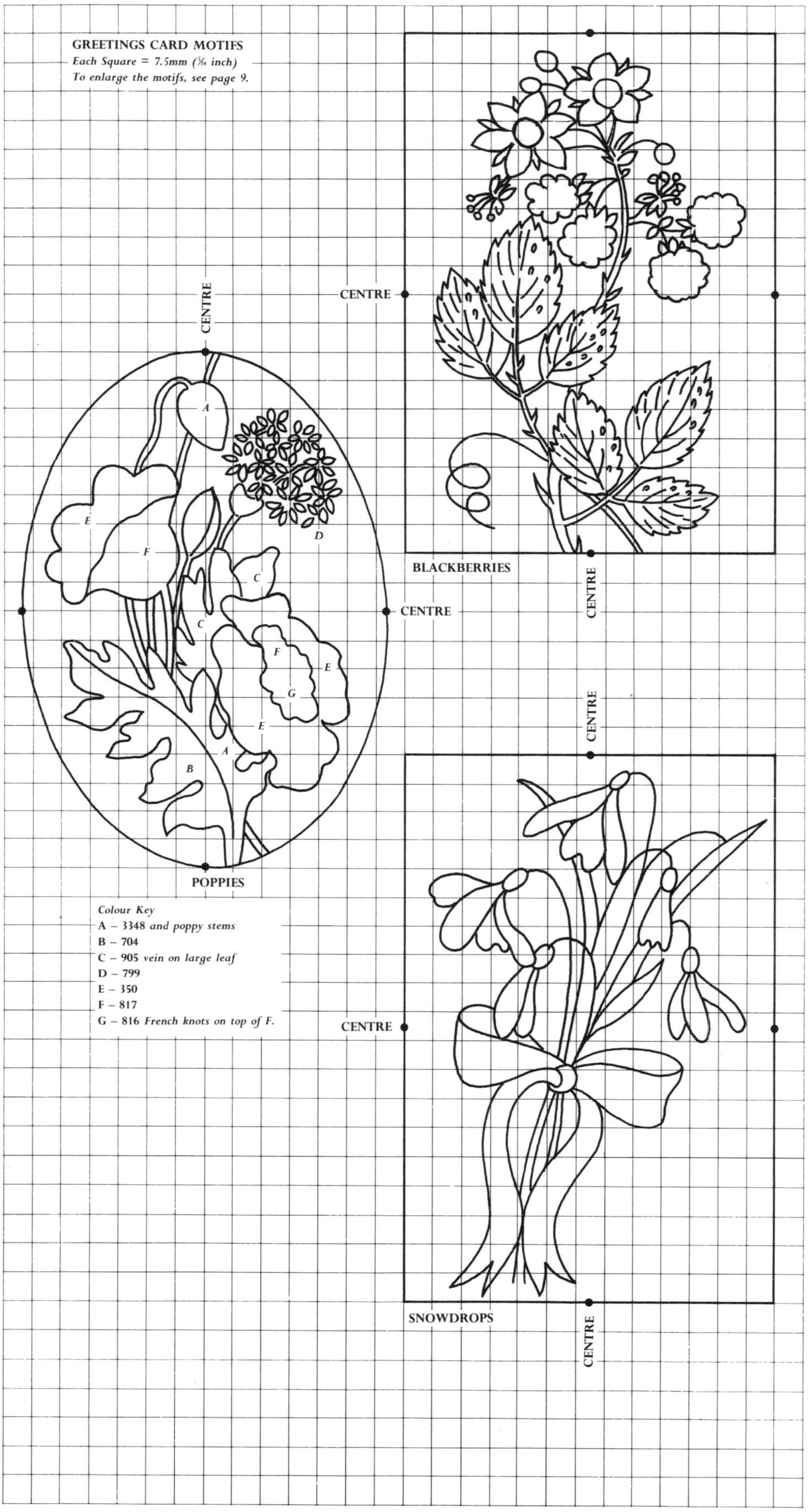
GREETINGS CARD MOTIFS
Each Square = 7.5mm (5/16 inch)
To enlarge the motifs, see page 9.
CENTRE
A
D
E
F
C
C
CENTRE
F
E
G
E
A
B
POPPIES
Colour Key
A – 3348 and poppy stems
B – 704
C – 905 vein on large leaf
D – 799
E – 350
F – 817
G – 816 French knots on top of F.
CENTRE
BLACKBERRIES
CENTRE
CENTRE
CENTRE
SNOWDROPS
CENTRE

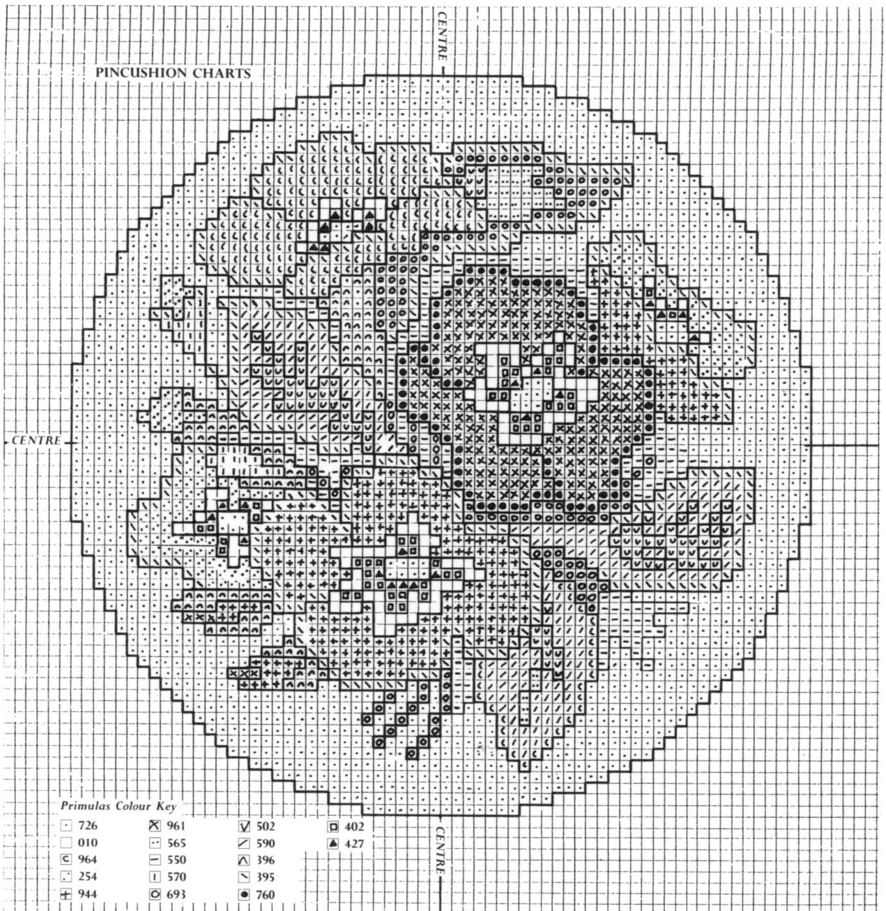
CENTRE
PINCUSHION CHARTS
CENTRE
Primulas Colour Key
726
010
964
254
944
961
565
550
570
693
502
590
396
395
760
402
427
CENTRE

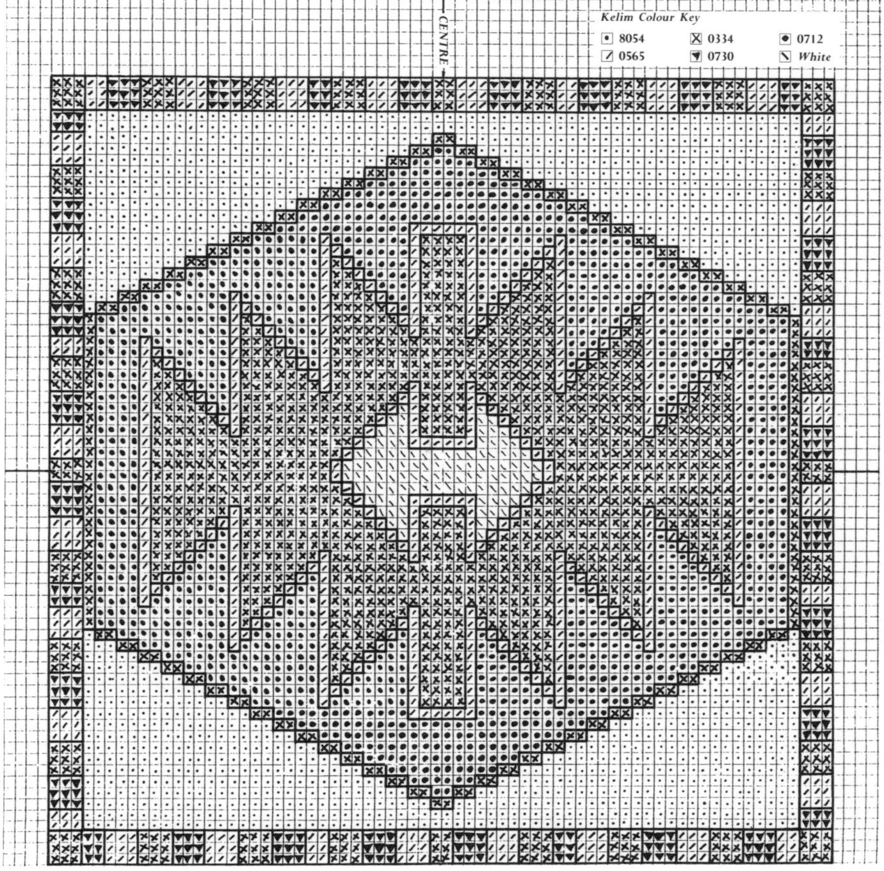
CENTRE
Kelim Colour Key
8054
0565
0334
0730
0712
White

P today
Happy Birthday
Holly

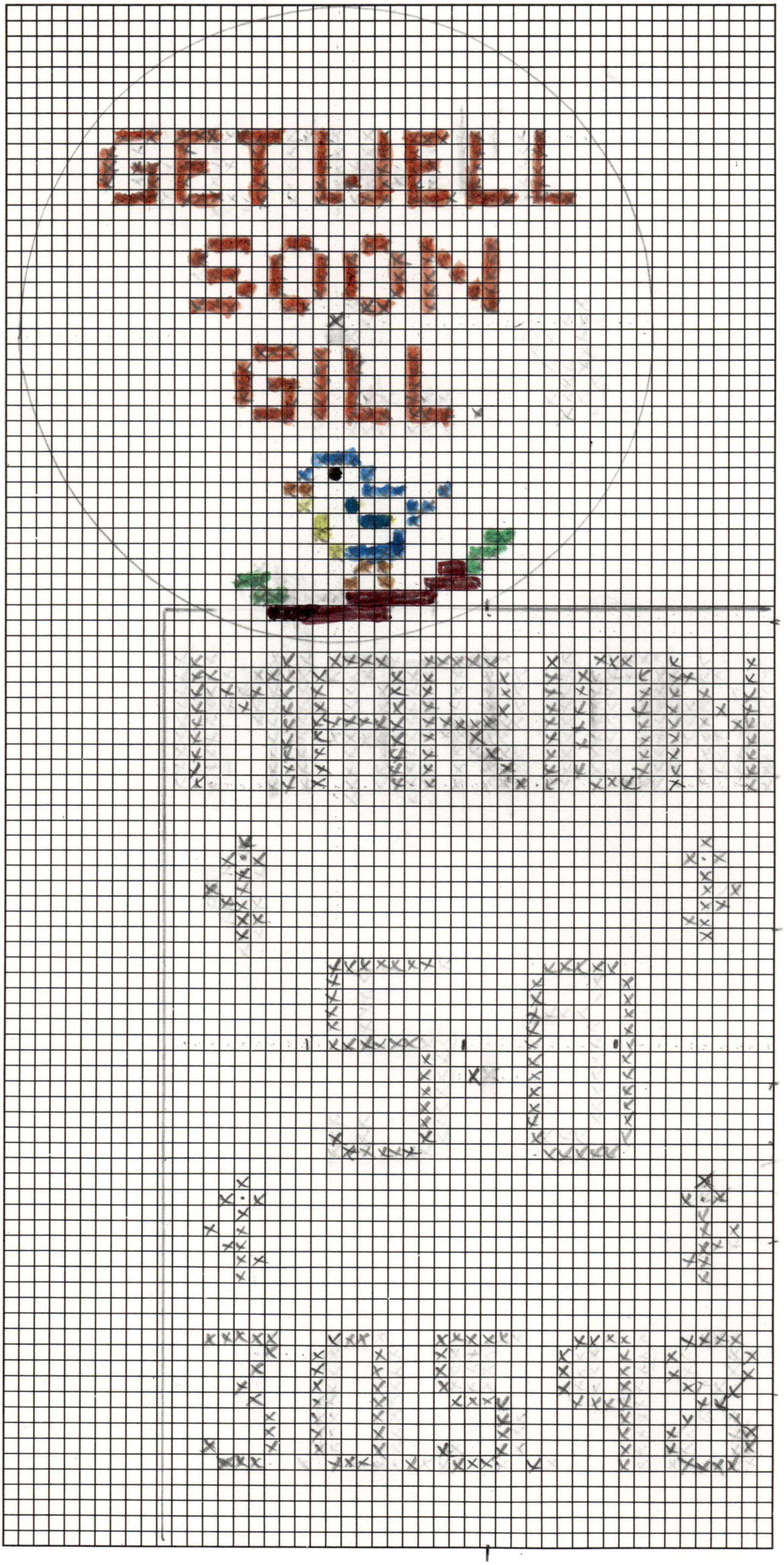
GETWELL
SOON
GILL

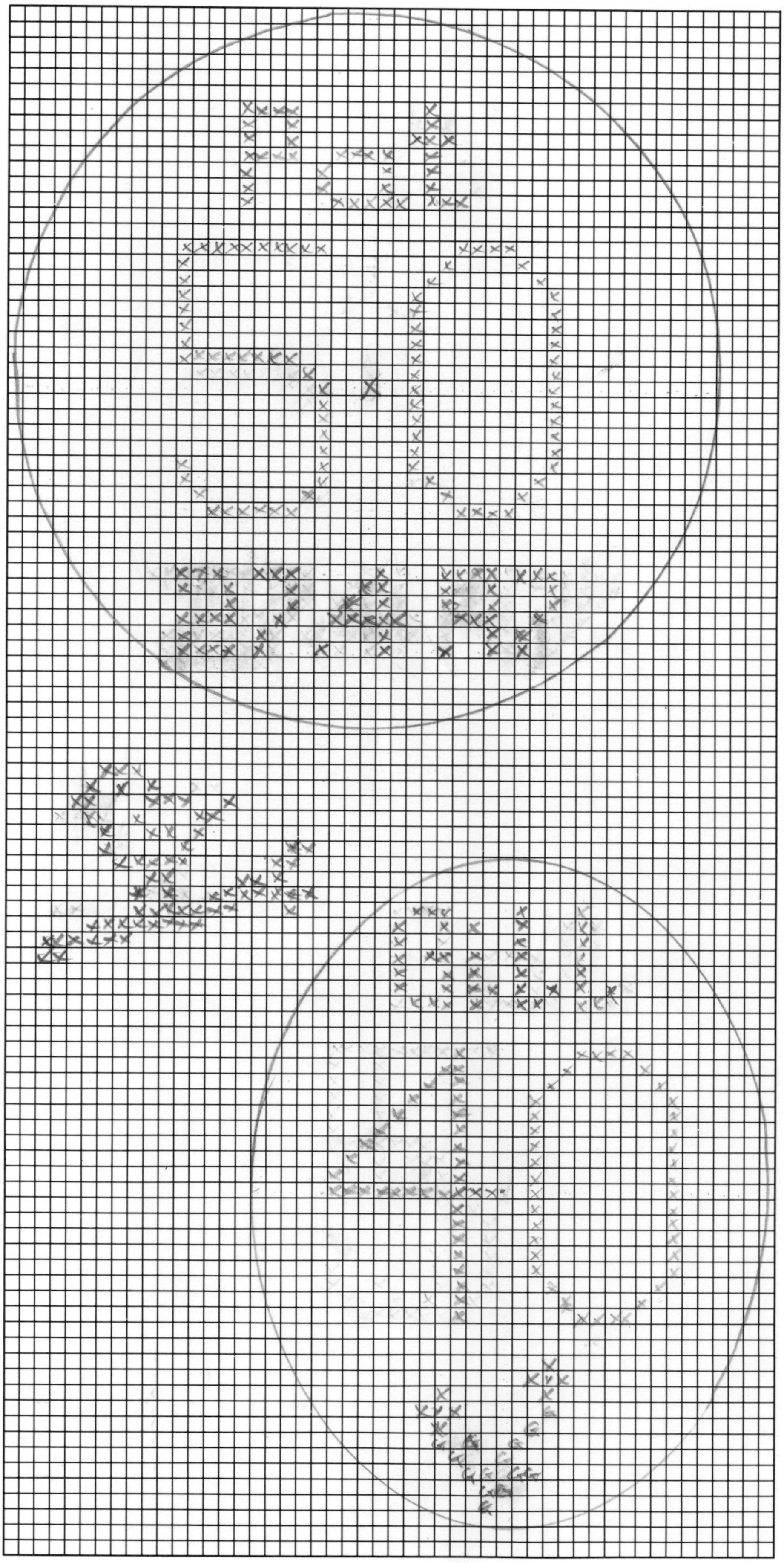

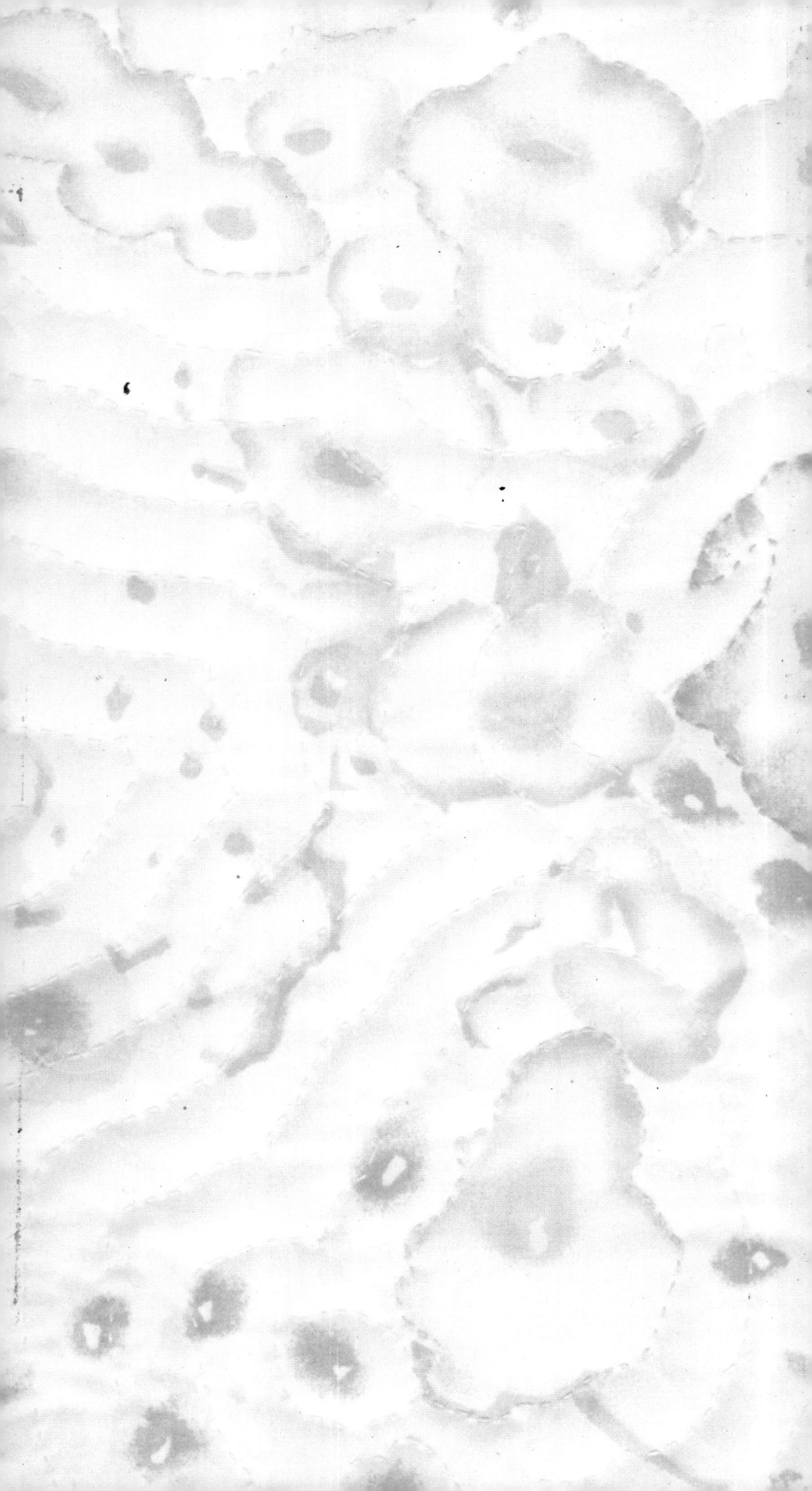